FUNERAL PLANNING MADE EASY

REGGIE-D

authorHOUSE®

AuthorHouse™
1663 Liberty Drive
Bloomington, IN 47403
www.authorhouse.com
Phone: 833-262-8899

Published by AuthorHouse   08/01/2022

ISBN: 978-1-7283-5797-3 (sc)

Print information available on the last page.

This book is printed on acid-free paper.

WARNING - DISCLAIMER

THANK YOU FOR BUYING MY BOOK

Literally, thousands of people, have benefited from the information, that can be found in this publication. If you are expecting to read an expose of the funeral service industry, forget that. Funeral Directors, as a rule, are honest, caring, hard working, considerate men and women, trying to make a living, like anyone else.

The information provided herein, is presented factually, and accurately, to the best of my ability. Of course, there are customs in parts of our wonderful country, that differ from other areas. I did my best, and will be the first person to admit, I'm not an expert. Also, it would be pure folly to think of myself as a writer. I hope we don't bore you to death. No pun intended.

I have more than 60 years experience, in the funeral service industry, but I don't claim to know everything. All in all, we feel that this book will be helpful to you, in planning whatever type of final service you desire, for yourself, or your loved one.

We have enjoyed providing you with this information. Please read each and every page, and then preplan your funeral arrangements. Discuss this information with your family members. Share the book with your friends.

Contact your local funeral homes, and get a price list from each of them. Compile all your vital statistical information, and write it down on the pages we have provided. Make an appointment to preplan your arrangements with your family funeral director. You will be amazed how easy it is when you are not under a lot of emotional stress. You will feel a great weight has been lifted off your shoulders.

This information has been compiled over a period of many years We hope you will be fortified with additional knowledge, to save yourself money, anguish, and heartache.

Our publisher's address is in the front of this book. If you have any questions, please drop us a line. We will try our best to assist you. If we get you on the right path, and help you save money with less anxiety, we will have achieved our goal.

I want you to know, that a percentage of the proceeds of this publication, will be donated to some of our favorite charities, and organizations. To name a few, The Girl Scouts; The Brownies; The Boy Scouts; The Cub Scouts, The Salvation Army; The Ministerial Associations, (which provide fuel oil, clothing, and food for the less fortunate); The Soup Kitchens, and Youth Athletic Organizations, for both Girls and Boys.

Thank you again, and God Bless,
Reggi D.

YOUR FAMILY FUNERAL DIRECTOR

Truly a unique individual. Can be male or female, and enters the funeral service industry for a variety of reasons. Some are following in their families footsteps.

Some have a sincere desire to help their fellowman through a difficult time in their lives. Some because it's a job, a livelihood.

Others because they think a funeral director/mortician is someone who sits around all day, dressed up in a suit, counting his money. These individuals don't stick around too long

For whatever reason, one chooses to become a funeral services professional, they soon realize that working in a funeral home becomes a 7-day, 24 hours, 365 day obligation.

Of course we are not working every minute of every day. We are on call most of the time, and are expected to stop what we are doing, and respond quickly. Death never takes a holiday.

Those of us who grew up in the family business, saw our parents miss meals and get called out of bed in the middle of the night. They had to interrupt party or social plans, and respond when duty called.

Ours is not the only profession or business that works around the clock, but many funeral practitioners never know what a 40-hour week is. They don't have every weekend off, and they know about working on Christmas or other holidays.

The beauty of all of this, is that rarely do we complain. Our inconvenience is mitigated by the grief and suffering experienced by the family that we~ are serving at that time. We jump into action to guide the family thru a difficult time.

Funeral directors must maintain high standards to be worthy of the community's trust. Many families have told us, that they selected us over other funeral homes in the area, because they have confidence in us.

Many families call the same funeral director, each time there is a death in their family, because they were treated fairly. They have established a high level of trust in the funeral director, because he or she cared about them. The funeral director tried to please them, and did his or her very best to carry out their every wish.

Funeral Directors, or Morticians, or Undertakers, as we are so designated in various states in the USA, generally wear two hats. First we are professionals, because we provide services. We are paid for our knowledge and experience. Secondly we are businessmen, and businesswomen, engaged in a very demanding occupation. You wouldn't believe the tons of paper work, and the many rules and regulations, that pertain to our profession.

We are governed by many city, state, and national rules, regulations, and laws. We are recognized and respected for our technical skills, and specialized services in caring for the dead.

Funeral Professionals are all trained to assist the bereaved, and guide them through a difficult time in their life. He or she knows what can be done, how to do it, with reverence and dignity. Since families have little or no knowledge in this area, your funeral director relies on his or her vast experience.

We understand the different religious customs, fraternal, special rituals, and military type services. Also, the many details required to have a loved one transported back home, when death occurs in another city, state, or foreign country.

All of these types of services are conducted with reverence and dignity. Since funerals are actually for the living, every effort is made to comfort the bereaved family.

The educational requirements to become a member of our profession, varies state to state.

First you are required to be a high school graduate. Some states require a college education, before you attend an accredited College of Mortuary Education. You must then secure a job at a licensed Funeral Home.

That funeral director will register you with the State Board, and you then are a Registered Apprentice. The funeral director will oversee your training, and see that you assisted on a minimum number of funeral services. Also, see that you assisted in embalming on a minimum number of bodies. The minimum numbers are dictated by the State Board.

You then are required to accumulate several credit hours of study, and graduate from a college of Mortuary Science. Some states allow you to serve your apprentice before, during, or after college.

The length of college education, and length of time you serve your apprenticeship varies from state to state. If you are interested in becoming a licensed funeral director, and you would like to know what the requirements are in your state, call some of the funeral homes in your area. They will be happy to provide the information you need.

Many men and women are entering the funeral service profession today. Those of us actively engaged, realized the need for continuing education, and higher academic training. We must maintain high Professional and educational standards to provide the various services to those families we serve.

Many states now require us to attend classes in continuing education This of course provides us with increased skills, and additional knowledge. We have a responsibility to serve our ever changing society.

The men and women in the funeral service industry today, are achieving professional and academic growth, in an ongoing learning program.

We take great pride in our profession, and have worked long and hard to secure and maintain our license.

It doesn't matter if you live in a small town, or a big city, you probably have met a Funeral Director. We are very involved in our communities You name it, and we are probably a member of that service club, fraternal, veterans, civic, political organization, in your community.

We work with little leagues, hospitals, hospice, high schools, the arts, boy and girl scouts, volunteer fire companies. The list goes on, and it only proves, that we want to be involved with our neighbors, our community, and help whenever we can. Service to others is a way of life for us.

Your family funeral director stands ready to assist you with your wishes. One of the smartest things you can do, is make an appointment with him or her to discuss your particular need. Also the costs associated with those items you are interested in. Listed below are some of the options open to you:

Traditional funeral services, with in ground burial, or entombment in a mausoleum;
Immediate or direct cremation;
Memorial Services;
Cremation with attended rites;
Immediate disposition or burial;
~ Donation of the body to your state anatomy board or medical college;
Military services, and burial in a National Cemetery or State Veterans Cemetery;
Pre-Need arrangements for yourself or loved one;
Transporting the deceased to or from your hometown, or another city;
Requirements needed for Protestant, Catholic, Jewish, and other religious services;
Memorial services for Masonic, Elks, Fire Companies, and other fraternal groups;
Securing Certified copies of death, birth, marriage or divorce certificates;
Medical Examiner and Coroner jurisdictions;
Caskets, and outer burial containers;
Cemeteries and Memorial Parks;
Obituaries, Florists, Organists, and Soloists;
Register books, memorial folders, prayer cards, and Thank You cards.

This is a partial list of services your funeral director has the knowledge and expertise with which to assist you. We will try to provide the answers to most of your questions on each of these subjects, as we go along.

With this information in hand, you will be able to make practical decisions, that will be just right for your particular needs. We want you to be an informed consumer. Knowledge is power. An educated consumer is a smart consumer.

VITAL STATISTIC INFORMATION

This is a very important chapter, the statistical information you give to your funeral director must be accurate. If you just guess, and provide inaccurate information, you are setting yourself up for problems in the future.

The information you provide is used for the Death Certificate, the obituary in the newspapers, your funeral director's records, and the State Department of Health, Vital Records or Statistics. The name of the state agency varies from state to state, but the purpose is the same. That being, the collection of vital and biographical information for all the citizens who are born, married, divorced, live and die in that state.

I won't go into all the reasons why the information must be accurate. I will say, however, that if the name of the deceased; or place and date of death; or place and date of birth, or the social security number, any one of these important items, are wrong you are going to have problems.

The first thing that comes to mind, is the Life Insurance Company. Incorrect info can cause a delay in the insurance check being issued, or in some cases being denied completely. Your funeral director can make corrections after the certificate has been submitted to the Health Department, but this requires a lot of time and work on your part, as well as the funeral director.

Keep in mind, your funeral director will gather this information from you in the arrangement conference, and some of it will be used for the death certificate, and/or the newspaper obituary.

Some newspapers use more information for the obituary, than others. I will outline the information used by the newspapers throughout our country, that put almost anything of interest in the obituary. This way you will be prepared with more information then you might need for your particular paper

As we outline the information needed, I will indicate what you can put in the obit. All newspapers have a certain format they use, and you generally can't change that. Some papers allow more latitude than others.

NAME OF THE DECEASED:--first-middle-last-Sr. Jr. Etc. FOR THE OBIT: you may use initials, and nickname, if it is in good taste.

THE ADDRESS:-- place of residence, house number, the street, the city, county & state. If the deceased has been residing in a nursing home facility for more than three months, most states require you to use the address of that facility for the official residence.

FOR THE OBITUARY:-- if the residence has been sold, or the deceased has resided in several places, you may put "formerly of _____," in the obit. Also, you might want to give some thought about leaving the address out of the obit, to prevent any robberies or vandalism when the residence is vacant while family members are away attending the visitation and/or services.

SOCIAL SECURITY NUMBER:- You must use the correct social security number for the deceased, not the spouse's social security number. NOT USED FOR THE OBITUARY.

VETERAN: If the deceased was a Veteran you need to provide which war, and/or dates of service. More on this important subject in another chapter. FOR THE OBIT: you need the branch of service, the unit, rank, dates of service. Awards, medals, and Theater of Operations, are also important.

MARITAL STATUS:--married-widowed-single-divorced. FOR THE OBIT: The spouse's name, date of marriage, years married. If the spouse is deceased, date of death.

EDUCATION:--number of years in school, including college. FOR THE OBIT: sometimes the name of the High School, the year of graduation, names of college(s), the year graduated, and degrees received. This also includes post graduate studies, and honors received.

RACE: WHITE BLACK HISPANIC OTHER NOT FOR THE OBIT.

OCCUPATION:---Type of employment---job description---not allowed to use retired, on the death certificate in most states. **FOR THE OBIT**: the name of a company, or government agency, office or position held, years of service, the year of retirement, awards received, honors and academic accomplishments. Owned and operated a business for a number of years.

DATE OF BIRTH: AGE: FOR THE OBIT:-- the age may be omitted from the obituary, if you so choose. This is done quite often, especially with deceased women, who are very secretive, or sensitive, about their age.

FATHER'S NAME:---first-middle-last-Sr. Jr. etc. FOR THE OBIT: ---is he living or deceased, and if newsworthy, some additional information about him, and his accomplishments:

MOTHER'S MAIDEN NAME:--first-middle-and last name prior to marriage to her husband. FOR THE OBIT: is she living or deceased, and if newsworthy, some additional information about her, and her accomplishments.

A note about the parents names Some people do not know the name of one or more of their parents, for one reason or another. If this is tile case, your funeral director will put "unknown" on the death certificate, and omit any reference to them in the obituary.

THE SPOUSE:---first-middle-last (if a woman, her maiden name is needed here.) FOR THE OBIT: -- same information as in MARITAL STATUS, above.

CLERGY:--- **ONLY FOR THE OBIT**: full name and title of Reverend, Pastor, Priest, Rabbi. Name, and address, of church, synagogue, temple, would be helpful to the funeral director.

PHYSICIAN:--The primary doctor who was taking care of the deceased. Name, address and phone number would be helpful, for the funeral director. NOT FOR THE OBIT.

CEMETERY:----name, the address of the cemetery. (Names of lot owners, who will be interred/ entombed next to whom. Is there a monument in place? This is helpful information for the funeral director.) FOR THE OBIT: name and address of the cemetery.

PLACE OF SERVICES: FOR THE OBIT:---funeral home, church, synagogue/temple, or in case of a grave side service, the name of the cemetery.

MEMORIAL DONATIONS:---in lieu of flowers, you need the name and address of church or charity, where the memorial donations are to be made, and a contact persons name and address. In some cases monetary contributions are requested for the benefit of a family, or more specifically, the children in a family.

It is desirable to use a bank or other type of financial institution as the recipient of the money. The public will be more generous in donating to a bank, than to a member of the immediate family. The perception is, the money will be better managed by someone at the bank, and will be used for it's intended purposes.

NUMBER OF CERTIFIED COPIES OF THE DEATH CERTIFICATE:---please refer to the chapter in this book, pertaining to certified copies, their cost, and the need for the same. You will then be able to tell your funeral director the number to order for you.

PALL BEARERS, OR CASKET BEARERS: ---see the chapter in this book pertaining to pallbearers.

LIVING SURVIVORS: FOR THE OBIT: some families like to list children by age. Others like to list the daughters, and then the sons. Spell all names correctly, list the child's spouse if you desire, and the city and state where they reside.

GRANDCHILDREN, GREAT GRAND, AND GREAT GREAT GRAND:---The same information as for the children. Spell all names correctly, and most families list by age, include spouses, and city and state where they reside. Some papers will not include the names of grandchildren, in the obit.

LIVING BROTHERS AND SISTERS:---The same information is needed, as for the children. Some like to list by age. Some like to list sisters, and then brothers. Spell all names correctly, list the living spouses, and city and state where they reside.

NIECES AND NEPHEWS: FOR THE OBIT: the newspaper will generally state "many" or "several" nieces and nephews also survive. Most papers will not list the nieces and nephews separately.

Some newspapers will list one or more special nieces, nephews, or friends. E.G., "He will also be remembered by a special niece, _____." or "She will be remembered by her fiancé_____."

NO BROTHERS OR SISTERS LIVING:---**FOR THE OBIT**: "he or she was the last surviving member of his or her immediate family."

DECEASED BROTHERS AND SISTERS: FOR THE OBIT: some papers will not include these names in the obit, but if they do, spell names correctly.

You have noted my concern about spelling names correctly. The information that you give your funeral director, is what will appear in the newspaper. If names are wrong, it creates problems and hard feelings among the family members.

Out of spite, some people will intentionally leave a relative or spouses' name out of the obituary in the newspaper. This is not a good idea, and just makes additional hard feelings.

CHURCH AFFILIATIONS: FOR THE OBIT:---Name of the church, synagogue, temple, etc., offices held, active in the choir, was a member of, or taught Sunday school. Also membership in mens or ladies clubs, circles, or bible classes. This can be omitted from the obit, or you can simply state, "he attended the Methodist (or whatever religion) Church.

MEMBERSHIP IN ORGANIZATIONS: FOR THE OBIT: Lodges, fraternities, or sororities, a fire company, a service club, political clubs, homemakers, bridge, golf, the military, etc. The offices held, life membership, awards, titles, educational background, unions, state and national offices held. Also many newspapers will list hobbies, e.g., bowling, hunting, fishing, knitting, sewing, gardening, etc.

Keep in mind, the obituaries are out there for the world to see and read. Your family funeral director will make sure that all information will be accurate, and in good taste.

Often, the family will ask us not to put an obituary in the newspaper. There is no law that states you must, and this is your choice to make. If for one reason or another you want everything very private, don't place the obituary in the paper.

Some obituaries are very long. They list the accomplishments of a very active person, and this is within the families right to do so. In the case of a paid notice, it would be expensive.

The basic purpose of an obituary, is to notify the public of someone's death. The time, place of the visitation and services, the survivors names, place of interment, and newsworthy information. You have many options available to you. You may put as little, or as much as you want in the obituary, consistent with the newspapers policy. **You make the final decision**.

OUTLINE OF VITAL STATISTIC INFORMATION

FOR THE DEATH CERTIFICATE AND THE NEWSPAPER OBITUARY

NAME_____NICKNAME_____

ADDRESS _____

SOCIAL SECURITY NUMBER_____RAILROAD RETIREMENT?:   Y   N

VETERAN: YES NO MARRIED WIDOWED SINGLE DIVORCED

OCCUPATION:_____ EDUCATION_____

DATE OF BIRTH:_____AGE:_____YEARS_____MONTHS____DAYS_____

PLACE OF BIRTH:_____

FATHERS NAME:_____ LIVING DECEASED

MOTHER'S MAIDEN NAME:_____LIVING DECEASED

SPOUSE:_____LIVING DECEASED

CEMETERY:_____STONE UP?: YES NO NEXT TO_____

OWNERS NAME:_____ SECTION_____LOT_____GRAVE_____

CLERGY:_____PHONE:_____

CHURCH:_____PHONE:_____

PLACE OF SERVICE: _____

PHYSICIAN: _____PHONE:_____

INFORMANT: _____RELASTIONSHIP_____

ADDRESS: _____PHONE: _____

MEMORIAL DONATIONS TO: _____

CERTIFIED COPIES OF CERTIFICATE: #_____STATE_____

BEARERS: (6) 1_____ 2_____ 3_____
4_____ 5_____ 6_____

ALTERNATES: _____

WAR: _____ SERVICE # _____ XC# _____ MARKER_____

ENTRY: _____ PLACE: _____ RANK_____

DISCHARGE: _____ PLACE: _____ BRANCE OF SERVICE_____

FLAG: YES NO   MILITARY SERVICE: YES NO   UNIT: _____

LIVING CHILDREN: SPOUCE CITY STATE

_____
_____
_____

GRANDCHILDREN   GREAT GRANDCHILDREN   GREAT GREAT GRANDCHILDREN:

_____
_____
_____

SISTERS/BROTHERS: SPOUSE   CITY   STATE

_____
_____
_____
_____
_____

DECEASED RELATIVES:_____
_____
_____

CLOTHING IS LOCATED: _____ GLASSES   ON OFF

HAIR: _____CALL: _____

PHOTO FOR LOCAL NEWSPAPER: YES NO   FOR HAIRDRESSER   YES NO

NAME OF NEWSPAPER(S) _____
_____

VISITATION AT: _____FAMILY ONLY/ PUBLIC

DAY: _____TIME: _____FAMILY ONLY/ PUBLIC

CASKET OPEN FOR VISITATION: YES NO   OPEN FOR FAMILY ONLY: YES NO

CASKET OPEN FOR SERVICE: YES NO   CLOSE 5 MINUTES BEFORE SERVICE: YES NO

CASKET OPEN AT CHURCH: YES NO   CLOSE 5 MINUTES BEFORE SERVICE: YES NO

VISITATION AT CHURCH ONE HOUR PRIOR TO START OF SERVIC: YES NO

FLOWERS IN CHURCH (WITH CLERGY'S PERMISSION) YES NO HOW MANY_____

LODGE/CHRISTIAN WAKE SERVICE AT FUNERAL HOME: DATE: _____TIME: _____

LODGE/MILITARY SERVICES AT CEMETERY: DATE: _____TIME: _____

TRANSPORTATION FOR FAMILY TO FUNERAL: _____
_____

FAMILY DISMISSED FOLLOWING SERVICE: FIRST_____ LAST_____

SPECIAL MUSIC: _____
_____

SOLOIST: _____

CLERGY TO ANNOUNCE FELLOWSHIP & REFRESHMENTS FOLLOWING SERVICE
(OR BURIAL) AT: _____

NOTES AND SPECIAL JNSTRUCTIONS: _____
_____
_____
_____
_____
_____

ATTORNEY & OTHER PERSONS TO CONTACT: _____
_____
_____
_____

OTHER IMPORTANT INFORMATION

IMPORTANT PAPERS   **LOCATION**

REAL ESTATE DEED _____

CEMETERY DEED _____

BIRTH CERTIFICATE _____

MARRIAGE CERTIFICATE _____

STOCKS-BONDS _____

TRUST FUND DATA _____

MORTGAGES _____

WILLS _____

INSURANCE POLICIES _____
_____

BANK ACCOUNTS _____
_____

PROMISSORY NOTES _____

CREDIT CARD ACCOUNTS _____
_____

CONTRACTS _____

GENERAL PRICE LIST:

In 1980, the **FEDERAL TRADE COMMISSION, (FTC)** made a list of rules and regulations, that all funeral homes/mortuaries, in the United States, must abide by. One of these regulations is the **GENERAL PRICE LIST**. Every funeral establishment must have this list of their charges, and provide them to people, when requested to do so.

We have listed each of the sections, followed by a general explanation, to help you understand the language used by the FTC. Your family funeral director will explain each item in detail, during the arrangement conference.

11

The **GENERAL PRICE LIST**, is also designed to protect the consumer. When you visit a funeral home, they must provide you with a complete up to date copy. It is my understanding, if you phone the funeral home and request a copy, the funeral director is not obligated to mail you a copy.

However, the funeral director will ask you to stop by his or her establishment, and will gladly give you a copy. As previously in this book, it is the policy of our funeral home to mail the caller a copy. We simply ask for their name, and address, and mail it to them. We are not alone in the practice, as many funeral homes do the same thing.

In recent years, the **NATIONAL FUNERAL DIRECTORS ASSOCIATION, (NFDA)** has conducted several surveys on the General Price List, within our membership.

This is a time-consuming process. It takes many months to mail the surveys, and gather the information. More time is needed to correlate the data, and arrive at the average cost, for each of the sections. Please remember, the figures we will be using, are just an average. Costs vary greatly, throughout the many different areas of our country.

Considering the time it takes to conduct this survey, the NFDA does a remarkable job in completing this task in a timely manner. NFDA's most recent General Price List Survey is based on figures as of January 2009, which are fees charged by funeral homes, in 2008.

Date collected is from 564 questionnaire responses out a total random sample of 1,500 NFDA members. This is an outstanding response rate of 38%.

The schedule of standard items are considered the average cost of an adult funeral. The respondents who participated in the survey, identified these standard items as those items selected by consumers more than half of the time.

This is 2010. Please keep in mind, the figures we will be using, were the average in 2009. They are provided for your information, as a rule of thumb. As a guide. Don't visit your family funeral director with the idea, that these prices will be current this day and age. They won't.

Unfortunately, in our society, prices go up, year after year. The cost of operating a business, regardless of the type of business, is an ever increasing demon. Your family funeral director is constantly aware of the rising costs he or she is faced with. They do the best they can, in keeping their prices as reasonable as possible.

Since the prices are always increasing, it makes good sense, to visit your family funeral director, and make arrangements for yourself, or your loved one. Paying for these arrangements, at today's prices, could save you hundreds of dollars, when death occurs, many years in the future.

The General Price List will state the name of the funeral home at the top of the paper. Under this, will be the effective date of the prices listed therein, also a statement that these prices are subject to change without notice.

The first section is: "**ITEMIZED SELECTIONS**" (We will list each section, using the language required by the FTC, followed by an explanation of each section.)

The goods and services shown below are those we can provide to our customers. You may choose only the items you desire. However, any funeral arrangements you select will include a charge for our basic services and overhead. If legal or other requirements mean you must buy any items you did not specifically ask for, we will explain the reason in writing on the statement we provide, describing the funeral goods and services you selected.

Explanation: "ITEMIZED SELECTIONS" It is important for you to understand, that you may choose the items you want. There are nine components of the most commonly selected items, which we will list for you. If you don't want to use one or more of them, you don't have too. As we examine each section, you will come to understand what services your family funeral director provides for you. You will also understand, that if you decline some of these services, which is your right, certain very necessary details will not be taken care of.

Any of the arrangements you select, will include a "non-declinable Professional Service Charge. You have to pay for this service charge. This charge is for basic services provided by the funeral director and his staff, and includes his overhead costs and expenses. We will explain this charge in more detail later.

As to the legal or other requirements that you are required to pay for, even though you did not specifically ask for these items. Your family funeral director is a professional, and is keenly aware of what can be done, ethically, legally and morally, and what can't be done.

Most of these situations will fall under the rules, regulations, and requirements of other agencies, such as the coroner, or medical examiner. Also, transportation to or from other states and foreign countries, memorial parks, cemeteries, crematories, oversized caskets, paid obituaries, etc., etc. Your family funeral director will explain these unusual situations to you honestly, and completely.

Each family we serve, presents it's own unique sets of circumstances. No two are exactly the same. The accommodations and services we provide, are too numerous to put in a price list.

1. BASIC SERVICES OF FUNERAL DIRECTOR AND STAFF:..............$2345.00

Our fee for the basic services of funeral director and staff includes, but is not limited to, staff to respond to initial request for service; arrangement conference with family or responsible party; arrangement of funeral; preparation and filing of necessary authorization and permits; recording vital statistics; preparation and placement of obituary notices; staff assistance prior to, during and following the funeral, including coordination with those providing other portions of the funeral, e.g., cemeteries, crematory and others. Also included in this charge are overhead expenses relative to our facility such as insurance, maintenance, and utility expenses, secretarial and administrative costs, and equipment and inventory expenses.

This fee for our basic services and overhead, will be added to the total cost of the Funeral arrangements you select. (This fee is already included in our charges for Direct cremations, immediate burials, and forwarding or receiving remains.)

Explanation: Most of these items are self explanatory. You might not know, however, that most obituaries placed in newspapers throughout the country, were composed by the funeral director. Of course they follow the format dictated by the newspaper, and in most instances the paper will print exactly what we send them.

This is the non-declinable professional service charge, referred to earlier. Also, there are many services provided by the funeral director, that are not mentioned in this section.

We like to compare the services provided for a traditional funeral, to that of a church wedding. Many of you have experienced the hassle and frustration, of planning, and coordinating a church wedding and reception.

In many instances, you need to start a year in advance, to reserve the church, clergy, a reception hall, a band, photographer, flowers, the caterer, etc. The six weeks immediately preceding the wedding, are particularly hectic.

Your family funeral director, and staff, has three or four days, or less, to arrange and coordinate, all the details for a traditional funeral service. Believe it or not, there are many more details to arrange a funeral, than a wedding.

The funeral director and his or her staff; perform these duties, efficiently, calmly, and with dignified professionalism.

2. EMBALMING: $850.00

Except in certain special cases, embalming is not required by law. Embalming may be necessary, however, if you select certain funeral arrangements, such as a funeral with viewing. If you do not want embalming, you usually have the right to choose an arrangement that does not require you to pay for it, such as direct cremation or immediate burial.

Explanation: Embalming is the art and science of disinfecting, preserving, and beautifying a dead human body for funeral purposes. If you don't want the body embalmed, It won't be embalmed. Simple as that. This is a declinable charge.

However, you will not be able to have an open casket, and perhaps not even a period of visitation. This depends on the funeral home's policy. Many funeral homes add an addendum to this section, which states, "our company policy requires embalming for public visitation."

One of our major responsibilities, is the guardian of the public health. There are many instances, when an unembalmed body, even when placed in a closed casket, would not be very pleasant during the visitation period. Also, under certain circumstances, it might be detrimental to the health of those in attendance.

If you choose direct cremation, or immediate burial, you do not need embalming. If you choose cremation with attended rites, then you do need embalming. This type of service, allows you to have a visitation, with an open casket, if that is what you want, followed by a funeral service. Then the body is taken out of the rental casket and cremated.

3. OTHER PREPARATION OF THE BODY:

A. This fee includes Cosmetology, Hairdressing, Grooming, Dressing and Casketing.. $ 325.00
B. Special care of Autopsied remains... $250.00
C. Washing and Disinfecting remains when no Embalming $325.00
D. Dressing and Casketing Unembalmed Remains $290.00

Explanation: A. This service is required when the body is embalmed, and the casket is L. open for viewing. Even if the family requests a closed casket, we have learned over the years, that 90% of the time, families change their mind, and someone in the family will want to view the remains. With that in mind, we make every effort to make the body look as presentable as possible. If the family tells us they have changed their mind, and would like to view the remains, we have no problem opening the casket for them.

This charge includes paying our staff hairdresser, or paying a hairdresser requested by the family. It is much easier, and better results are achieved, when the family gives us a photo to use. Cosmetics are lightly applied, and the clothing placed on the remains.

Casketing, is placing the body in the casket. This is not as easy as it sounds. It is very important that the body appear to be resting comfortably. This helps create a pleasant memory picture.

Some remains are difficult to position because they are terribly misshapen, due to injury, disease or old age. Then there are the extremely overweight people. Sometimes you wonder if they are going to fit in a regular size casket.

B. Without going into much detail, an autopsied body requires much more time to embalm, than remains that are not autopsied. The embalmer is faced with certain situations, that place him or her in harms way, considering the various types of killer diseases we are faced with today. Embalming autopsied remains, requires a greater amount of expensive chemicals and supplies, to achieve the desired results.

Some funeral homes do not charge the family for this service. Ours is one of them.

C. The remains are thoroughly washed with a medicinal soap, and then treated externally with disinfecting solutions. It protects the members of the funeral home staff when handling the remains. Also, this protects members of the family when viewing the unembalmed remains, prior to cremation, or interment. If the funeral home permits a period of visitation, with an unembalmed body in a casket, this charge would apply. There could be a private family viewing, but no public viewing.

D. This charge would include the services in item C., plus, dressing and positioning the unembalmed body in the casket properly. Here again, there could be a private family viewing, but no public viewing.

4. USE OF FACILITIES FOR VISITATION:

A. Use of Facilities and Staff Services For Visitation (two hours). Our services include Setup of visitation area, placement of encased remains; display of floral arrangements, supervision of and attendance during the visitation. ....$ 595.00
Additional hours of visitation would be... $ 100.00 per hour

B. Equipment and Staff Services For Home, Or Church Visitation (within 20 miles)
This includes a casket bier, and any other equipment needed for visitation, plus setup, placement, and display of floral arrangements .... $ 595.00

Explanation: a. This charge is self explanatory. It is also declinable. If you don't want a period of visitation, the day or night prior to the funeral, you have another option. You could arrange to have a visitation one or two hours prior to the funeral service, at the funeral home.

b. A lot of labor and time involved in this arrangement. The casket bier, kneeling rail, register stand, flower stands, chairs, lights, and other equipment is needed. All of this necessary equipment must be transported in a large vehicle, such as a van. Some funeral homes, include the use of this motor vehicle in this charge. Others make a charge for the van.

If you are having the visitation in a private home, keep in mind the dimensions of the door leading into the building. It must be sufficiently wide enough to accommodate a casket. You also need room inside, to maneuver the casket to the proper location.

If there are steps leading to the building, several men will be needed to carry the casket into the residence. Another important factor is, plenty of parking is needed for visitors calling to pay their respects.

Churches usually have a parking area for visitors. Many of the older churches have built ramps into the church, to comply with the American Disability Act, (ADA). This may eliminate the need for any extra manpower to get the casket into the church.

(20 miles) This is generally the funeral home's service area, but varies with different funeral homes. Transportation over the 20-mile radius could result in a mileage charge to the family. Most establishments are very flexible about this 20-mile radius.

5. USE OF FACILITIES FOR FUNERAL:

A. Use Of Facilities And Staff Services For Funeral Service, Or Additional Staff Necessary For Service In Other Facility. Our services include coordination of the funeral arrangements, supervision of funeral and staff to attend funeral ceremony $595.00

B. Same charge for coordination and supervision of Church ceremony ....$ 595.00

C. Same charge for coordination and supervision of Grave side service ....$ 595.00

D. Use of Facilities and Staff Services for Memorial Service (without body).

Our services include accompaniment of the memorial service arrangements, supervision of the memorial service, and staff to attend the service .... $ 595.00
Memorial Service at Church, or Grave Side .... $ 575.00

Explanation: A. Self explanatory. If you decide to eliminate the visitation, the day or night prior to the funeral, you can have visitation one or two hours prior to the funeral. There should not be any additional charge for the visitation period.

B. This would also apply, if the tl.ineral ceremony was held at Church.

C. This would also apply for a Grave side service.

D. This Memorial Service is held when the body is not present, generally after direct cremation. Sometimes this is a service held for a family member, that died and was interred in another state, or country. Also, the remains were never recovered, e.g., lost at sea.

6. TRANSFER OF RFMAINS TO THE FUNERAL HOME:

A. Within 20 Mile Local Service Radius $595.00

B. Additional Miles Outside Local Service Area (Cost per mile one-way) ....$ 3.50**
**additional fuel charges may apply

C. Additional Personnel for Residence Removal ....$ 75.00

Explanation: A. One of the most important services we funeral directors provide, is the removal of the remains, from the place of death. We must respond quickly, anytime, 24 hours a day, seven days a week, 365 days a year, in alt kinds of weather conditions.

As mentioned previously, the 20 Mile Local Service Radius, is somewhat flexible.

When death occurs in a hospital, the response is normally delayed several hours, or a day or more. The delay might be caused by organ and tissue donation, or an autopsy. One of the most frustrating delays, is caused by waiting for the physician to sign the death certificate. Holidays, and weekends are another factor, because some of the medical, and support staff are off duty. Getting the Pathology Department to do an autopsy in a reasonable time during these holiday, and weekend periods, almost requires an act of congress.

In all fairness to the physicians, we realize they have very busy schedules. They might not be able to sign the certificate for many hours following death. Some physicians will have their associate sign the death certificate, if he or she was familiar with the deceased's condition All in all, funeral directors have a great relationship with the physicians in their area.

Most hospitals will not release the remains to the funeral home, until the physician has signed the death certificate. This is true for general hospitals, state and veterans facilities.

Any delay caused by organ donation, autopsy, or failure to secure a signed death certificate, causes problems in making definite funeral arrangements. We hesitate to put an obituary in the newspaper, notifying the public of visitation and funeral arrangements, until we know for certain when the body will be released.

The response time for removing the remains from a nursing center, is fairly quick. Most nursing homes don't have an area to isolate the deceased, so we go to the deceased's room.

There might be several other patients in this same room, with the deceased. Our policy is to have the nurse show us exactly which patient we are to remove. If it is in the middle of the night, and the lights are low, many of these poor souls appear to be dead. It would be a horrible mistake to remove a patient who is still alive. We have been told, that this has happened more than once, through carelessness, of all those involved.

Most nursing homes, will allow the funeral home to make the removal, and have the death certificate signed by the physician, later that day, or tl1e next.

Deaths resulting from vehicular accidents, murder, suicide, abortion, drownings, etc. fall under the jurisdiction of the Coroner or Medical Examiner. Sometimes rescue and ambulance personnel, transport the remains to a morgue, or hospital when directed by the police. Especially those remains that are laying outside, or in a public place.

In some states, funeral homes also participate in making these removals. They usually alternate with other establishments, on a rotation basis. Depending on the number of funeral homes that choose to provide this service, they each could serve for 30 days at a time. They are paid a small fee by the State, for this removal service.

The Medical Examiner, or Coroner, the Forensic Investigators, and police agencies, know which funeral home is on call, for that month. They immediately know whom to call.

Something that you should be aware of: **YOU HAVE THE RIGHT TO CALL THE FUNERAL HOME OF YOUR CHOICE**, if you are ever in this type of situation.

For example. A family member dies, or is killed, and the ABC funeral home has made the removal, because it is their month to be on call for the Medical Examiner. A representative of the ABC funeral home, telephones you, and informs you they have made the removal of your loved one. They ask you, when it would be convenient for you to come to their funeral home and make the necessary arrangements. They lead the family to believe that their loved one is in the funeral home, when it actually is in the hospital, or morgue.

This is ethically, and morally wrong for the ABC funeral home to do this. It is also illegal. They know that the family is in a state of shock, and will be under the impression that they must make arrangements with the ABC funeral home.

You **DO NOT** have to deal with this particular funeral home, if you don't want to. It is within your right to call another funeral home of your choice.

If this is the only funeral home that serves your area, then you don't have much choice in the matter. They probably have served your family in the past, and will do their very best to accommodate you.

If however, you are called by one of these "ambulance chasing" firms, you should write a letter to the **STATE BOARD OF FUNERAL DIRECTORS,** in your state. Do this after a period of mourning. The funeral home of your choice, that handled your loved one's arrangements, will provide you with the address of the State Board.

Funeral directors that prey on the emotions of people in a crisis situation, have to be stopped. These people are also the individuals who bribe others to steer business their way. Some funeral directors offer money, and gifts to individuals who are in a position to recommend one funeral home over another.

Nothing will be done to stop this unethical practice, unless the general public complains to the proper state agencies. They must be prevented from taking advantage of other people in similar situations. It isn't fair to the families, nor is it fair to the other ethical funeral homes in your area. Please excuse me for getting up on my soapbox.

A funeral director told me about a conversation, he had with a very active member of the 1-lospice group, in his county. It seems that one of the care givers in this 1-lospice organization, was approached by a local funeral director. The funeral director, as the story goes, offered money, if the care giver would refer his funeral home to the families, she served.

The Hospice organization put a stop to this quickly, and handled everything quietly. There was no publicity. Some said that Hospice should have publicized the incident. Hospice should have made the public aware of what the funeral director tried to do. Others told me that this would have done a lot of good for Hospices' outstanding image in their community.

Many funeral homes throughout the country, use a "Removal Service," to transport remains to their funeral homes. Some of these removal firms, located in the large metropolitan cities, serve so many funeral homes, that they handle more than 10,000 cases in a year.

The removal service company has one or more vehicles to transport remains. Usually, these are vans, that can make a removal from a residential development, without attracting much attention from the neighbors.

Employees of these companies, are both male and female. They are strong, courteous, well mannered, and maintain a caring attitude. After all, they are representing a local funeral home, and must make a good impression. They know their way around the various hospitals, and nursing homes. When on duty, they respond all hours of day and night, and in all types of weather conditions.

One of the services provided by a removal service company, is to transport remains long distances. They will travel to distant cities, to deliver or pick up remains, at another funeral home. It's common for some of these companies to be in airports, on a daily basis.

The equipment they use, is very expensive, but necessary to accomplish their tasks. One-Man mortuary cots, cost more than $1800.00 each, and they own several of them.

Also, they have cot covers, heavy duty and disposable pouches, body scoops, Reeves stretchers, rubber gloves, and sheets, to name a few. Their vehicles, are expensive to purchase, and maintain, especially with all the Department of Transportation guidelines they must follow. Insurance costs are out of sight.

B. The mileage charge of $3.50** per mile one-way, when required to travel beyond the 20-mile service area, is self-explanatory. Remember. This represents the charge three years ago. It may be double that in 1999. **fuel surcharge may apply

C. The charge for Additional Personnel For Residence Removal, is also a legitimate charge. Making a removal from a hospital, or nursing center, usually requires one person.

Removal from a residence is another story. Some funeral homes, make a charge for an additional staff member to assist on the removal. This is at all hours, day or night.

Sometimes it is necessary to enlist the assistance of ambulance or fire & rescue personnel to remove extremely large remains from a residence. Family members are always willing to help, and that is greatly appreciated, but not expected.

Perhaps death was the result of a suicide, homicide, natural causes, or the remains are extremely large. We need help in removing the body from the place of death, in a dignified manner.

7. FUNERAL COACH: (Add $3.50** each mile outside 20-mile service radius)

A. Funeral Coach (Hearse)..$ 475.00

Explanation: A. A funeral coach, or hearse, as it is commonly called, is a very expensive piece of equipment for a funeral home to own. Not only is the purchase price, (prices can easily exceed $ 100,000.00), out of sight, but the maintenance costs are very high.

Most small funeral homes do not own a hearse. They have an agreement with a "Livery Company," to provide them with a hearse, when needed. This is a great deal for the funeral home. The funeral director gets a clean, late model hearse, complete with a competent driver.

A livery company might just provide hearses and limousines. However, most of these livery companies, also provide removal service. They serve several funeral establishments in their area. At the time of death, they deliver the remains to the funeral home. On the day of the funeral service, they return with a hearse, and transport the body to the final resting place.

Funeral coaches are usually Cadillacs, Lincolns, Buicks, Pontiacs, Chevrolets, and believe it or not, Mercedes Benz. Many of these coaches are available in many colors, such as gray, white, blue, maroon, green, and the traditional black, to name a few.

Like limousines, they may have one color on the roof, and another on the body of the hearse. Most have vinyl tops, and these come in various shades and colors.

Back in the days when funeral homes were providing emergency and routine ambulance service, the vehicle of choice was a combination hearse, and ambulance. One vehicle, which provided two entirely different services, to the families they served.

The vehicle was usually setup as an ambulance, for quick response to a call for help. The side windows in the rear, were emblazoned with a red cross, and white stripes etched in the glass. Inside, the floor was smooth and flat, easy to keep clean.

A special type hook was securely attached to the inside rear wall of the vehicle, on the drivers side. This was necessary to hold the stretcher/cot in place while the vehicle was in motion. A quick release leaver was activated, to remove the cot from the ambulance.

Two sections of the floor, directly behind the front seats, flipped open to provide seats for two attendants, or passengers. A siren was hidden from view under the hood, which was activated by a switch near the dashboard. A flashing or revolving red light was attached to the roof, toward the front of the vehicle.

A special type hook was securely attached to the inside rear wall of the vehicle, on the drivers side. This was necessary to hold the stretcher/cot in place while the vehicle was in motion. A quick release leaver was activated, to remove the cot from the ambulance.

Two sections of the floor, directly behind the front seats, flipped open to provide seats for two attendants, or passengers. A siren was hidden from view under the hood, which was activated by a switch near the dashboard. A flashing or revolving red light was attached to the roof, toward the front of the vehicle.

For many years, funeral directors provided emergency and private ambulance service to their communities. This is still true today, in many remote areas of our country. The people that provided this service in the past, and those who still do, have my deepest respect, and admiration.

As they say, "Been There, Done That!." For more years than I care to remember, our firm provided ambulance service. We had members of our staff, and part -time helpers, that specialized in this service, but it seemed like I was working with them all the time. This was in addition to my duties as a funeral director, and embalmer. We were much younger then.

When we needed this vehicle for a funeral service, it only took a few minutes to convert. The red light was removed from tl1e roof. The ambulance cot taken out, and stored in the garage. complete with sheets and blankets, ready to use.

Panels on the floor were flipped over, and we then had a floor with rollers, for the casket to roll on. The casket stops were then put in place, to prevent the casket from rolling around, when the hearse was moving.

These rollers were on the underside of the flat, smooth, Formica type floor, when used as an ambulance. The cot holder was usually left in place, as it was against the wall, out of the way.

Next two large panels were placed over the rear side windows, to hide the red cross, and other emergency markings. The exterior of these panels was painted the same color as the vehicle. Each had a landau bar on it, to represent the old time carriages.

In a matter of several minutes, one person can change this single vehicle, from an ambulance, to a hearse, or vice versa. They were called "combination coaches," and they were just the ticket for any size funeral home. It eliminated duplication in purchasing, and maintenance, and upkeep.

A few times, when it was converted to a hearse, and in use on a funeral, we were called for an ambulance transfer. We simply called one of the other funeral homes in our community,

Thank heavens for the well trained, well-equipped ambulance personnel we have today. Emergency Medical Technicians, (EMT), Medical Response Teams, Fire and Rescue Departments, and Medivac type helicopters.

These men and women provide a great, very efficient service. A thousand percent improvement, over the old days. I for one, am very glad they are providing this service, and we aren't. They are saving lives every day, and that is just wonderful.

8. FLOWER VEHICLE, SERVICE OR LEAD CAR, AND LIMOUSINE:

A. The flower vehicle, is usually a van, or suburban style truck. Large enough to accommodate the floral arrangements, and transport them to the cemetery. Quite often, the family asks us to deliver some of the flowers to nursing homes. If this flower vehicle is not needed, then the family is not charged for it. This would be a declinable charge, when not needed.

It is also used to transport equipment needed for a visitation, or service, at a church, or residence. It is a very important multipurpose vehicle.

B. Service or Lead Car. We use this sedan, to go to the physicians' office, newspaper office, and Bureau of Vital Records to get certified copies of the death certificate. In other words, it is for business related errands.

For the funeral or memorial service, we call for the clergy person, and transport them to the place of service. When the service is over, we use this sedan to lead the funeral procession to the cemetery, taking the clergy person, and some of the pallbearers. Following the committal service at the cemetery, we transport the clergy person back to the church or parsonage.

C. The Limousine is one vehicle, that doesn't fit into the budget of many funeral homes. Many families like to drive their own cars, as individual family units. It makes it easier to leave directly from the cemetery, go to a place of fellowship, or their separate ways.

Like us, many funeral homes, have a Limo that they've had for years. They are in excellent shape, but they are very seldom used. Many of the average income type people, feel it is too pretentious, to ride in a limousine. They feel as if they are showing off.

9. MEMORIAL MERCHANDISE:

A. Register Book .... $ 60.00
B. Memory Cards .... $ 50.00
C. Prayer Cards ....$ 60.00
D. Acknowledgment Cards (*per box*) ....$ 35.00

Explanation: A. The Register Book, is a guest book, placed in the visitation and f funeral service areas. Those family members and friends, in attendance, sign this book, so the immediate family will be able to refresh their memory as to who was there. This book is cherished by many families, and looked at repeatedly, in the coming years.

Register books are available in many colors, and styles. Many are designed for a specific religion, or fraternal organization, or veterans group, and infants, just to name a few.

They may be very inexpensive, with a simple paper cover, or have a cover of padded vinyl, that would be moderately priced. Also available, is a large wood covered register book, with elaborate embossing, which is very expensive. We decided not to offer this particular book to our families, because it was too expensive, and due to its size, would not fit on our register stand.

B. Memory Cards, or Memorial Folders, are placed in the visitation and funeral service areas, usually close to the Register Book. The outside of this small folder, portrays most any type of outdoor scene, religious, floral, fraternal, military, occupational or athletic picture you could imagine. They are very beautiful, and are designed to be peaceful, and perhaps portray a small glimpse into the deceased's beliefs, occupation, or activities, during his or her lifetime.

Inside the folder, information about the deceased is printed on the right side. Date of birth, date of death, day, time, place of services, and the name of the clergy.

On the inside left, a scripture verse, short poem, prayer, or memorial message, is printed. Some funeral homes now have the capability to reproduce a photo of the deceased on this left side, above the verse. Many people keep these memorial folders in their family bible.

We have seen some of these, and they are very nice. This provides a very nice keepsake. They are perfect to mail to family members and friends, who were unable to attend the services. We understand the equipment needed to produce the photos on memorial folders, is not cheap.

C. Prayer Cards, are usually placed on a special stand, near the casket. They have a beautiful photo on one side, of Jesus, Mary, Joseph, or many other Saints, and religious Icons, On the opposite side is a special Prayer, and the name of the deceased, with the year of birth and the year of death. These Prayer Cards are provided for those in attendance, along with Mass Cards. Just like the Memorial Folders, they are keepsakes, and, again many people keep them in their bible.

D. Acknowledgment Cards, are also known as Thank You Cards. They are engraved with a message of appreciation, and are available in hundreds of styles. Boxed in quantities of 25 or 50, they come with an equal number of envelopes. Some styles are designed so you can open them, to write a personal message, inside. Families mail the cards, to other family members and friends, to thank them for acts of kindness, they may have provided the family. They express their appreciation, for gifts of money, food, flowers, sympathy cards, use of vehicles, serving as a casket bearer, and many of reasons.

All four of these items, listed under Memorial Merchandise, are declinable, if you choose not to pay for them. You may choose any, or none of them.

Some families use their own Register Book, or Guest Book, and some prefer to use their own thank you notes. Ninety-five percent of the families however, will use all of these memorial items, because the funeral director has them readily available. They are beautifully designed for this particular purpose, and reasonably priced.

THE GENERAL PRICE LIST, CONTINUED:

In addition to the nine basic services, previously listed in this book, your family funeral director will have the following services outlined in the General Price List.

The language used, is required by the FTC, so that all funeral director's price lists outline the same basic services. Some funeral homes rearrange their General Price List, a little, but they all are basically the same. Of course, the prices for these services, will vary with each funeral establishment, and some firms will offer Package Deals. They combine several services, and offer them to the public at a lower price, than if they were selected separately.

The prices we used, as an illustration, for the previous basic services listed, were based on the NFDA's survey, as of January 2009. Remember, the survey was actually based on fees charged by funeral homes, in 2008.

The NFDA has not provided us with survey results, for the types of services we will now outline for your information. With this in mind, we will be using current charges made by funeral homes. To the best of our knowledge, these prices will represent an average of funeral home charges in 2010.

FORWARDING REMAINS TO ANOTHER FUNERAL HOME:

This charge includes, removal of remains, basic service of staff, embalming, necessary authorizations, and local transportation to the airport. This charge does not include visitation, rites or ceremonies prior to forwarding of the body.

A. With Minimum Shipping Container ....$ 4,387.00

B. With Casket Selected From Our Funeral Home
(addition to the cost of the casket) ....$ 5,337.00

C. Combo-Air Tray ....$ 250.00

Explanation: A. This type service is needed, when someone dies in one community, and the family want the remains shipped to another community. The family contacts a funeral home in community "A." We will call him the receiving funeral home.

This funeral director or the family, calls a funeral home in community "B," and requests the remains be prepared, and shipped to the receiving funeral home. We will call firm "B" the shipping funeral home.

The shipping funeral director receives vital statistic information from the receiving funeral director. The removal is made from the place of death, the necessary permits secured, and the remains are embalmed. The remains are then encased in a Combo-Air Tray.

A Combo-Air Tray, (Combination-Air Tray) is a shipping container, constructed of particle board, and heavy duty cardboard. It is a container that provides dignified protection of the remains, for shipping by air, when a casket is not used. Straps hold the top section, securely to the wood base, and the Burial-Transit permit is secured to the top section.

This container is approved, and required for shipping, by all the airlines. It may only be used one-time, according to airline regulations.

Generally, all Other Preparation, such as dressing, cosmetics, and hair dressing, will be provided by the receiving funeral home. Many times the family will purchase the casket, from the receiving funeral home.

The charge of $ 4,387.00, for item "A" includes $ 200.00 for the Combo-Air Tray.

B. If the family, for one reason or another, wishes to purchase a casket from the shipping funeral home, the price of the Combo-Air Tray will be deducted from the $ 4,387.00.

The charge is now $ 4,187.00. ($ 4,387.00 less $ 200.00) A casket is selected by the family, and this charge is added to the $ 4,387.00.

When a casket is used, the airlines require the shipping funeral director, to encase the casket in an "Air Tray." This is constructed with a wood bottom and a heavy cardboard section that covers the casket completely. Straps hold the top section, securely to the wood base, and the Burial-Transit Permit, is secured to the top section.

The cost of the Air Tray is $150.00. Like the Combo-Air Tray, it is approved and required by all the airlines. Due to airline regulations, it may only be used once.

The shipping funeral home makes all the airline reservations, and notifies the receiving funeral home. The information related will include, the name of the airport, which airlines, the Flight Number, day and time of arrival.

The airlines all make a charge for the transportation of human remains. Depending on the arrangement between the shipping and receiving funeral homes, the remains may be shipped "Pre-Paid" or "C.O.D." If shipped "C.O.D.," the shipping funeral home, provides a letter, guaranteeing payment of the air cargo charges. This is a routine procedure, that all funeral homes are aware of.

RECEIVING REMAINS FROM ANOTHER FUNERAL HOME

This charge includes local transportation of remains to cemetery and basic services of staff This charge does not include visitation, rites or ceremonies.
(Grave side service only) .... $ 3,160.00

Explanation: This type of service is needed, when a funeral home delivers the remains to the receiving funeral home. The remains are usually embalmed, and encased in a casket.

There will be no visitation, or funeral service at the funeral home, or church. Transportation is provided to a local cemetery or mausoleum, where services are held.

The receiving fimeral home makes all arrangements at the cemetery, and secures the clergy person, requested by the family. The receiving funeral home will place the obituary in the local newspapers, if the shipping funeral home has not already done so. If not already arranged, an outer burial container will be purchased by the family.

Many times, the family will want more than a Grave side service, and request a period of visitation, and a funeral service, at the funeral home, or church. The receiving funeral director will make all the necessary arrangements, and add the appropriate charges to the Statement of Funeral Goods and Services.

If the family doesn't want to pay for a period of visitation, they could arrange for a period of visitation, one or two hours prior to the funeral service. This is a money saving option.

The family will have the usual options, as to accepting or declining the Memorial Merchandise, e.g., Register Book, Memorial Folders, etc.

If the receiving funeral home is required to travel to an airport, to receive the remains, there will be a mileage charge for that service

Also, family members who might be traveling by air, might need transportation, to the community where the services will be held. It would be less expensive for them to rent a car from a car rental agency, then to pay the funeral director for transportation.

Local transportation might be needed by family members, on the day of the funeral service, and possibly a flower van. The charges for these vehicles will be added to your statement by the receiving funeral home.

We have tried to summarize the services you might need, when shipping to or from one community, to another community. Your individual situation, and the various services needed, might be much different. We hope we have provided you with enough information, to assist you in making practical decisions.

IMMEDIATE BURIAL

This charge for immediate burial includes local removal of remains, local transportation to the cemetery, necessary authorizations and basic services of staff. This charge does not include the use of facilities and staff for any visitation or ceremony, public or private, prior to burial. No embalming, and lightweight body pouch. (Our Company policy: Burial within 36 hours)

A. Immediate Burial With Casket Provided By Purchaser ....$ 3,999.00

B. Immediate Burial With Gray Cloth Covered Soft-Wood Casket
Selected From Our Funeral Home ....$ 4,949.00

C. Immediate Burial With Casket Selected From Our Funeral Home
(In addition to cost of the casket) ....$ 3,999.00

Explanation: A. The services provided for Immediate Burial are self-explanatory. Since there is no embalming, the remains are placed in a lightweight pouch. With the services included in item "A," the family has the option of providing the casket.

B. With this option, the family may purchase a Gray Cloth Soft-Wood Casket from the funeral home, for $ 600.00. Added to the basic charge of $ 1,845.00, for the Immediate Burial, the total would be $ 2,445.00.

C. If the family wants a type of casket other than the one offered in item "B," they may purchase a casket from those offered by the funeral home.

In addition to the selections, listed above, there are other expenses you should be aware of.

If you don't have a burial site, it will be necessary to purchase one. The cemetery will also make a charge for opening and closing the grave.

Most cemeteries require an outer burial container. You can purchase a vault or liner from your family funeral director. if your local newspaper makes a charge for the obituary, you will need to ask your funeral director to put the obit in the paper for you. Most newspapers will not accept information for an obituary, from anyone, other than the funeral home personnel. You can pay the funeral director for the obituary charge.

if you want flowers, you can order them from the florist. If your plans include a clergy person to officiate at the grave site, you will need to give the clergy an honorarium. Since there will be no visitation or funeral ceremony at the funeral home, you do not need to purchase any items of Memorial Merchandise, e.g., Register Book, Memorial Folders, etc.

DIRECT CREMATION

The charge for a direct cremation includes removal of remains, local transportation to the crematory, necessary authorizations, basic services of the staff, and the crematory fee. This charge does not include the use of facilities and staff for any visitation or Ceremony, public or private, prior to cremation. If you want to arrange a direct cremation, you can use an alternative container. Alternative containers encase the body and can be made of material like fiberboard or composition material, with or without an outside covering. The containers we provide are plastic pouches, or a gray cloth covered casket.

A. Direct Cremation with container provided by purchaser .... $ 2,990.00

B. Direct Cremation with plastic pouch ....$ 2,990.00

C. Direct Cremation with gray cloth covered casket selected from our
funeral home ....$ 3,940.00

D. Direct Cremation with casket selected from our funeral home (in addition to the cost of the casket) ....$ 2,990.00

E. Mailing cremains to cemetery or a funeral home .... $ 150.00

F. Medical examiner fee .... Quoted when needed

Explanation: A. Those families who select immediate or direct cremation, come from all religious and social backgrounds. We hear many reasons for this choice of final disposition, ranging from their concerns about the future scarcity of burial space, to lower prices.

For whatever reason families choose cremation, they still have many options available to them. They may choose to have cremation with attended rites, which includes visitation and funeral ceremony, or immediate for direct cremation.

Your family funeral director will tell you in the arrangement conference, that you do not need embalming. You will also be informed, that if you choose direct cremation, you do not need to purchase a casket.

Crematories generally will not accept remains, that are not encased in a suitable container. The reason being, to protect their employees, and reduce the risk of contamination, and infection. Item "A", listed above, allows the purchaser the option, to provide a container of their own choosing.

B. If it is not convenient for the purchaser to provide a container, then we move to option "B". This particular funeral home, offers a plastic pouch, which meets the necessary requirements of the crematory, and only costs $ 150.00. Other firms choose to use a heavy duty cardboard container, called a "cremation tray." These are offered to the family, for $ 125.00 to $ 150.00.

C. Some families prefer to use a casket, which is made of a soft wood, and is covered with a gray cloth. The additional cost for the casket ….. $ 990.00.

D. Families that prefer to use a casket, and don't want to use the gray cloth type, may select a casket from those offered by the funeral borne. The basic charge of $ 2,990.00, is added to the price of the casket selected. The price of the casket could range from several hundred to several thousand dollars,

E. Quite often we are asked by families, to mail the ashes of their loved one, to a funeral home or cemetely~ in another part of the country. This is done through the United States Postal Service, and mailed 'Priority Mail." Many people are not aware that cremated remains are shipped in this fashion, but it is done many times, each day. They are bandied with care and dignity, and to the best of my knowledge, they haven't lost one yet.

The crematorium puts the ashes in a plastic bag. The bag is placed in a heavy duty cardboard box. The container is then taken to the Post Office, and the appropriate postal charges paid. This price list above indicates this charge to be $ 150.00, which includes postage.

F. In many cities across our country, the Coroner or Medical Examiner, must countersign the death certificate, if the remains are to be cremated. They make a charge for this service, which varies from city to city. Most of the charges in our state, and surrounding areas, average about $ 75.00 to $ 100.00. Time, mileage and fuel charges are the detennining factors.

Cremation is a process, that uses extreme heat to reduce the human body to small bone fragments, and some enamel off the teeth. Depending on the type of retort, or furnace used, this process takes about four hours. This includes the warming up, and cooling down periods.

There is a large amount of line granules and dust. The larger bone fragments are made smaller, by putting them through a grinder, or pulverizing machine. These ashes, or cremains, as they are often called, are placed in a plastic bag, with a metal disk. The metal disk has the cremation number, the name of the deceased, and dates of birth and death. This is required by law, for identification purposes.

These cremains will be buried in a cemetery, scattered, placed in a beautiful urn to be displayed at home, or placed in a mausoleum niche. Unfortunately, some are left at a funeral home, perhaps, never to be called for. We have several containers, that were left with us many years ago.

PRENEED PLANNING

One of the most important things you can do for a member of your family, yourself, or a dear friend, is preplanning funeral arrangements. Making plans for the future.

It is much easier to make rational and practical decisions, if the person is still alive, than after they have passed away. There is considerably less emotional distress. When you have finished making these arrangements, you will feel like a great weight has been lifted off your shoulders.

After death has occurred, you, or several members of the family meet with the funeral director to make arrangements. There are many questions that you might not know the correct answer to. Also, since these decisions have been suddenly dropped in your lap, you may not be absolutely sure of what type of service the deceased really wanted, or can afford.

Planning prior to death gives you an opportunity to discuss these items in advance with the individual, and secure all the information needed. Also, you can pay for these services in advance, if you so desire. It could save you money in the future.

These days, most nursing homes, after admitting your loved one into their nursing facility, will ask you to contact your family funeral home, to make preneed arrangements. The nursing home also wants the name of your funeral home on file, so they know who to contact when the patient dies.

The nursing home will also recommend that you secure an "Irrevocable Trust Agreement" after you pay for the funeral arrangements. This is especially important, if you are planning on your State Department of Health or Human Resources, (the name of the state agency varies from state to state) to eventually pay for the patient's care at the nursing facility, when the patient runs out of money.

Your Social Services Representative will explain all the details to you. Usually they want you to provide them with what seems like a ton of financial information about the patient. You will need to provide this state agency with all bank records, dating back two or three or more years. This includes savings and checking accounts, CD's., real estate property owned, life insurance policies, stocks and bonds, and burial plots in the name of the patient.

To qualify for state assistance to pay for nursing home care, when the patient's money is gone, this complete financial profile of the patient's assets is needed, dating back several years. The Irrevocable Trust Agreement you execute with the funeral director, removes money you have paid the funeral home from the patient's financial profile. It is irrevocable. It cannot be returned.

However, it can be transferred to another funeral home. The money doesn't belong to the patient. It belongs to the funeral home. For example, if you paid $ 8,890.00 for a complete funeral, that $ 8,890.00 is not counted as an asset by the state agency, when they are establishing the patients financial profile. The same is true if you paid $ 2,990.00 for your funeral arrangements, or any dollar amount.

The state will need a "Statement of Funeral Goods and Services Selected" from your funeral director. This shows the type of service you have purchased. It must be receipted Paid In Full.

Also, your state will require a copy of the "Irrevocable Trust Agreement" fully completed, signed by all parties, and witnessed. In states where this trust agreement is required, all funeral directors have copies of this simple, but most important document.

Some states have a limit on the amount of money you can prepay a funeral home for funeral arrangements. Just ask the state representative who is assisting you with your application. They will advise you, every step of the way.

A word of caution, for those states that do not have a limit on what you can prepay. Beware of any funeral director who advises you to set aside an exorbitant amount of money for funeral expenses. For example. Let's say the funeral director recommends that you put $25,000.00 or more in a prepaid funeral trust agreement, with his funeral home. The idea being, he will refund you a portion of that money at the time of death.

This is very wrong. It is illegal, and unethical. The IRS, as well as other government agencies take a dim view of this fraudulent transaction. All parties involved could be in serious trouble, with a capital "T."

It might sound tempting to escrow 25 or 35 thousand dollars, and at the time of death, and receive what you perceive to be a tax-free refund of 10 or 15 thousand dollars. Also, you might be paying more for that funeral service. It could actually cost several thousand dollars less, just because of the slick manner in which this fraudulent deal was presented to you. If you want my advice. **DO NOT PARTICIPATE IN THIS TYPE OF SCHEME.**

Some funeral arrangements, with certain types of merchandise selected, can indeed cost the consumer 15 to 30 thousand dollars or more. if that is what the consumer wants, they are willing to pay for it, and there is no refund at the time of death, that's fine.

It is not our place, meaning you and me, to be judgmental about what people pay to bury their loved ones. I personally have never made arrangements that cost any ways near that much. There are many people however, that will pay thousands of dollars, just to bury their pets. Different strokes for different folks.

In the preneed planning conference, your family funeral director will discuss many options available to you, and secure biographical and statistical information. He or she, will explain the prices for the different services they provide. Don't hesitate to discuss with the funeral director all of your wishes, and concerns. For example:

Do you want embalming?
Do you want viewing? Private family viewing or public viewing?
Do you want a visitation, and when?
Do you want the casket open or closed?
How much do caskets cost?
How much do outer burial containers cost?

What types of caskets and outer burial containers are offered?
Do you want the services held at the funeral home, church, or gravesite?
Do you want a Mass at the church?
Do you want an evening Christian Wake or Vigil service at the funeral home?
Flow much do Prayer Cards cost? Will there be Mass cards available?
Flow much do Register Books, and Memorial Folders cost?
How much do acknowledgement cards (thank you cards) cost?
Will we receive a temporary grave marker? Is there a charge for it?
Do you want to be cremated?
Do you want a Memorial Service? If so, where?
Do you want cremation with attended rites?
How much do Urns cost? Do I need an urn?
Do you want to donate your body to medical science?
What Clergyperson, Priest, or Rabbi do you want to officiate?
Can the funeral director secure a Clergyperson, Priest, or Rabbi for us?
Do you want a Military service at the gravesite?
Do you want fraternal or lodge services? Where and when?
Do you want an evening Fire Company Memorial service at the funeral home?
Whom do you want for pallbearers? Can the funeral home provide bearers?
Do you want friends to send flowers, or make donations to a church or charity?
What type of flowers do you want on your casket?
What will your family need in the way of cars or limo's for the funeral?
In what newspapers do you want the obituary to appear?
Do you want a photo in your local newspaper?
Do you want photos and other memorabilia around the casket for visitation?
What cemetery or mausoleum will be used?
If for a woman, who is to style her hair? How much make up?
If for a man, what about his beard, sideburns or mustache?
Where will the funeral director secure the clothing needed?
How much should the family pay the Clergyperson, Priest, or Rabbi?
How much should the family pay the Organist? Soloist?
How much are Mass, and other church fees?
Do you plan to have a period of fellowship and refreshment, after the service?
Where will this he held? Will the clergy invite family and friends for you?

How many certified copies of the death certificate are needed?
How much do they cost?
Will you be able to get additional copies in the future?
Who will transport the excess floral arrangements to nursing homes, or churches?
Who will get the small floral arrangements and vases after the service?
How soon can the family visit the gravesite, later that day?
What happens to the flowers that are placed on the grave?
How long will the tent remain over the gravesite after the burial?
Will the pallbearers wear gloves or boutonnieres?
What type of special music and what soloist will be wanted?
Will the family be dismissed first or last at the conclusion of the service?

These are just some of the things for you to think about prior to your appointment with your family funeral director.

We will discuss many of these items in this book. Please study them, and make notes. Write down all your wishes, and questions on a piece of paper. Discuss the various options with your spouse, and other family members.

When you meet with your family funeral director, you will have all your ducks in a row, and it will make it much easier for you to accomplish your goals.

Remember. These arrangements are for you, or a member of your family. Don't be bashful, be determined, and make sure your family funeral director knows exactly what you want, and what you don't want. After all, you are paying the bill, and it will be very comforting for you to know, that you will get exactly what you paid for. You can trust your family funeral director.

Your funeral director will appreciate the fact that you are informed, prepared, and well organized. It will make it much easier for the funeral director to accommodate you, and carry out your wishes

We haven't listed any type of service that is unusual, or difficult to provide. Most funeral homes will be very happy to answer all your questions. You will find that they routinely provide many of these services. If you feel that you are not happy with what the funeral director tells you, thank him or her for their time, and go to another funeral home.

It is much easier to change funeral homes when you are discussing prearrangements, than if you wait until death has occurred. You are not under as much stress, and there is no need for urgency to make these decisions. Also, if you want to save money, go ahead and pay for everything. It's like the man on TV says, "you can pay me now, or you can pay me later." We all know, that by paying later, could mean we will be paying more. Much more.

IF DEATH OCCURS OUT OF TOWN

Unfortunately people do die when on vacation, business trips, and traveling out of their home area. Also, people, who have retired, and moved to another state, or have relocated because of their employment, or a million other reasons.

TRADITIONAL FUNERAL SERVICES:

Let's take the individual, who has moved his or her residence to another locale. The first thing you must decide, are you going to have visitation and services in the new location. Have you resided in the new area long enough that you have many friends in the area. Perhaps, you might have many relatives living there.

If you do, and you feel that it is important to give your new friends an opportunity to share their grief with you, then you should call a funeral director in your new hometown. This of course, will result in some duplication of costs, because of the two funeral homes involved.

If you haven't, for one reason or another, had an opportunity to make friends in your new area, then you should call your funeral director in your former hometown. (This is also true in the aforementioned situations, when the deceased was traveling out of his or her home area.) This is probably the area where you have family, and most of your friends live. This is most likely the community where the cemetery is located, where you will bury your loved one.

All funeral homes have access to several Nationwide Shipping Services. These professionals will assist your hometown funeral director. They take care of all the necessary details, to transport your loved one back home quickly, and at a reasonable price.

Your hometown funeral director will get some basic information from you, and then call the Nationwide Shipping Service. They in turn will contact a funeral home that represents them in or close to the city in which the death occurs. This firm will make the removal from the place of death, secure the necessary signed certificate, and Burial-Transit Permit, and take care of the necessary preparation. They will place the body in a container called a "Combination/Air Tray".

This is required by all Air Lines for transportation of human remains by air. This combo/air tray is constructed of plywood and cardboard, and can only be used one time. This is a regulation established by the air lines, to insure your loved one will be handled safely, and with dignity.

The funeral director will transport the body to the nearest airport, and ship it C.O.D. to your hometown funeral director. Your hometown funeral director will meet the plane at the airport, and transport the remains to the funeral home, ready to carry out your instructions.

- The Nationwide Shipping Services all charge approximately the same fee for their services. They in turn, reimburse the funeral director in the community where death occurred. —Your hometown funeral director will make sure that you will not be billed twice for the same services. Of course, you must reimburse your hometown funeral director for the air line charges.

Some times death has occurred within your hometown funeral directors driving area. If that is the case, their will be no need for the combination/air tray, or transportation by air.

Your hometown funeral director will drive to the other funeral home, and transport your loved one back to your hometown. Our firm will generally drive up to 500 miles one-way. Our charge for transportation for this long trip, will be less than the cost involving one of the Nationwide Shipping Services.

Our charge for transportation, will also be less than the cost of a combination/air tray; air fare, and the shipping funeral home's charge for transportation to the shipping airport. The charge made by the receiving funeral home to transport the remains from the airport to his or her establishment, would also be eliminated. Cost wise, it is less expensive for the family, if their funeral director will make the trip, instead of involving other firms.

CREMATION SERVICES:

Let's say that the death occurred out of town. Regardless if the deceased was a resident in the new area or not, it is the families wish to have immediate or direct cremation. The practical, and less expensive plan of action, would be to call a funeral home in the area where the death occurred. They will carry out your wishes.

Feel free to phone your hometown funeral director for any advice or help, he or she can give you. We all have directories, listing addresses and phone numbers for every funeral home in the United States, and most foreign countries. Your family funeral director will gladly provide you with the information that you will need.

CREMATION WITH ATTENDED RITES:

When this type of service is desired, and death has occurred out of your funeral directors service area, please refer to the section on the preceding page, pertaining to Traditional Funeral Services. Call your hometown funeral director to take charge of all details for you.

Even though you plan to have cremation, instead of burial or entombment, your hometown funeral director will need to provide most of the services of a traditional service.

If death occurs more than 500 miles from home, your funeral director will call a Nationwide Shipping Service, or another funeral home in that area, to return the remains home. All the services provided will be the same as for a traditional service, with the exception of renting a casket. Cremation will be the final disposition, instead of burial or entombment in a mausoleum.

By calling your hometown funeral director, you will be avoiding duplication of charges for services. You could save a lot of money.

CASKETS:

The selection of a casket is one of the most important decisions a family makes, in the funeral arrangement process. It can also be somewhat confusing, because of your emotional state of mind, and your lack of knowledge of such things. Also, there are many to pick from, which adds to your confusion.

However, with the able assistance of your family funeral director, you can select a casket that will be very beautiful, and fit into your particular price range.

We are going to discuss the various styles and price range of caskets. We sincerely hope that you will become more knowledgeable about this part of the funeral process, and become an educated consumer. Again, we stress the importance of pre-planning these arrangements, in advance of the death of a loved one, or yourself.

TYPES OF CASKETS:

Basically, there are just two types of caskets. Metal and Wood. Both types come in a wide variety of styles, colors, quality, and prices.

METAL CASKETS:

There are three types of metal caskets. Bronze, Copper, and Steel. Bronze offers the finest quality and protection, followed by Copper, Stainless Steel, and Steel.

Bronze is an alloy consisting chiefly of copper and tin. It has been used for several thousand years, starting with tools and weapons, during the Bronze Age. It has been widely used for sculptures and other works of art. When used outside, as gates and doors of large buildings, it withstands the ravages of weather beautifully. Over time it develops a beautiful patina, and color. It will never rust or corrode.

Caskets made of solid Bronze, are a work of art. They are very impressive, and are very heavy. A 48 ounce Bronze casket, will be constructed of a sheet of solid Bronze, that weighs 3 pounds, per square foot. Likewise, a 32 ounce Bronze casket, will consist of a sheet of solid Bronze that weighs 2 pounds per square foot.

Considering the many square feet of solid Bronze needed in the construction of a casket, you have a considerable amount of weight.

Copper is a reddish-brown, malleable, metallic element. It is an excellent conductor of electricity and heat, and it's uses in our everyday life are numerous.

A casket made of solid copper, will usually consist of a sheet of solid 32 ounce copper. This tells us, that each square foot of copper, weighs two pounds. Copper caskets are very beautiful, and also heavy.

Copper, like Bronze, will never rust or corrode. A perfect example of it's enduring quality, is the Statue of Liberty, which has been standing out in the New York 1-larbor for many years. The outer covering of the Statue of Liberty, is solid copper.

Recently the steel skeleton inside her copper outer covering had to be replaced. The steel had rusted and deteriorated, terribly, because of the moisture, and weather conditions. The copper outer layer of the statue was still in great condition. It was removed, and simply replaced over the newly built steel inner structure.

Steel is a hard, tough metal composed of iron, alloyed with small percentages of carbon, and other metals such as nickel, chromium, and manganese. This produces a metal that is durable, and resistant to rusting.

The standard of measure for Bronze and Copper used in the manufacturing of caskets, is "ounces." The standard of measure for steel used in the manufacturing of caskets, is a "gauge."

Twenty gauge steel will measure 1/20th of an inch thick; 18 gauge 1/18th of a inch, and 16 gauge will measure 1/16th of an inch. This is the standard used to measure the thickness of steel.

The smaller the number, the thicker, and heavier the steel. Therefore a sixteen gauge steel casket, will be stronger, and heavier than an eighteen or twenty gauge steel casket.

Stainless Steel is another excellent quality material, that is used to make caskets. Stainless steel is steel alloyed with chromium and other metals, making it virtually immune to rust and corrosion. You can find it used in kitchens, for sinks and countertops, in your home.

Metal caskets are divided in two categories, Protective and Non-Protective. Protective caskets can be identified by a rubber gasket that helps seal the top of the casket with the bottom. It is engineered in such a way to prevent the entrance of water, air, and other gravesite substances, into the casket.

Non-protective caskets do not have this gasket or sealing mechanism, which make them slightly less expensive than the protective type.

Bronze, Copper, Stainless Steel, and your heavier gauge steel caskets, are generally designed as Protective Caskets.

Many of the twenty, or nineteen gauge steel caskets are in the non- protective category, but so are some 18 gauge caskets. It's confusing, but the manufacturers, know what the needs of various funeral homes are, and they supply that need.

Let's discuss the Non-Protective casket. First of all, it is made of steel. I have never heard of a Bronze, Copper, or Stainless Steel casket, being non-protective. Also, cloth covered particle board, and wood caskets, are non-protective, unless a bronze or copper, hermetically sealed inner unit, is placed inside the casket. More on that later.

Non-protective steel caskets come in a variety of gauges, styles, and colors. They are pretty, and very practical. They are, in some cases, less expensive than protective caskets. If this is the type of casket that fits into your price range, you need not be afraid to buy it. If the protective aspect bothers you, you can expect to receive excellent protection in a vault.

Protective caskets, or all types, have a rubber gasket that helps seal the top to the bottom of the casket. Rubber, as you know, will never deteriorate under ground. That is one of the reasons, we can't bury our used automotive rubber tires, underground.

The various sections, that make up the top and bottom of the casket, are electro-welded together, to form water resistant seams. Many of these caskets, especially those made of steel, are treated with an undercoating, that is far superior to the undercoating, used in the manufacturing of automobiles. This helps make them resistant to the entrance of air, water, and gravesite substances.

Many coats of the finest quality of paint available, are applied. There are some styles of bronze and copper that are also painted. When I was much younger, I couldn't understand why a beautiful copper casket would be painted. I have always liked the copper penny, brushed finish, on a solid copper casket The new colors are absolutely beautiful. Many firms will show three solid copper caskets, in their casket selection room. The traditional copper finish, plus a blue finish, and a white with pink finish.

Caskets come in almost any color imaginable. They are painted in solid colors, two-tones, highlighted with many shades, and have metallic, stippled, and brushed finishes.

Many manufacturers will completely immerse these caskets in a vat of water, and pump air under pressure, inside the casket. If any bubbles surface, the casket is examined, and the problem corrected. The casket will not pass inspection, if there are any bubbles surfacing, during this test.

Some manufacturers apply a chemical inside the casket, that was developed by the Dupont Corporation. This helps prevent the possibility of the casket rusting from the inside, due to the normal decomposing of the remains, over a period of tune.

The Belmont Casket Company, many years ago, manufactured a lead coated, or lead lined casket. This was a beautifully crafted casket, and was very distinctive. Some models have a round or elliptic end, and they were very popular with families.

Prices of metal caskets: Bronze is usually the most expensive, followed by Copper, Stainless Steel, and the Steel. There is some overlapping, with protective and non-protective steel caskets. Sometimes you will find heavy gauge steel non-protective steel caskets, that are priced less than lighter gauge protective steel caskets. Your family funeral director will explain the difference in the price of caskets in his or her casket selection room.

The people in our society, are growing taller, and getting much heavier. This creates problems with positioning remains in the casket, so they look comfortable. When it is impossible to place someone in a standard width casket, we need to use what is called an oversize casket.

Oversize caskets are available in various extra widths, and extra lengths. They of course, are more expensive, than a comparable casket that is standard in width or length.

When it is necessary to use an extra wide or extra long casket, a domino effect is created. The outer burial container and the size of the grave opening will also have to be wider and/or longer. This of course will be an added expense in both instances.

Your family funeral director carries in stock, or has photos of Infant and children's caskets. Also, the funeral director will have, or can order orthodox caskets, needed for families of the Jewish faith.

Wood Caskets: Some families like the warmth and natural beauty of wood. Maybe the deceased loved the forest, or woods, or perhaps they were a carpenter, cabinet maker, or worked with wood. Whatever the reason, wood is a very popular, and beautiful type of casket.

The species of wood used, will dictate both the cost and appearance of the casket.

Most common types of wood used for caskets are listed below in the order of expense:

Walnut, followed by Mahogany are the most expensive.

Cherry, Maple, Oak, and Ash, with the least expensive being Poplar and Pine.

As previously noted, wood caskets are included in the non-protective category, unless you purchase a bronze or copper, hermetically sealed inner-seal, which is placed inside the wooden casket. The inner-seal will be resistant to the entrance of air, water, and gravesite substances, but not the wooden casket.

Wood caskets are also available in extra widths, and extra lengths. The interiors of wood caskets, are similar to interiors used in metal caskets. They can be made of velvet, crepe, or satin, and are available in many different shades and colors.

Many caskets today, including both metal and wood, have some type of theme, or illustration, in the inside of the lid. There are many types, e.g., Praying Hands, Chapels and Churches, Doves, Sea Gulls, Streams, Mountains, famous people, like Rev. Martin Luther King, President John F. Kennedy, and his brother Robert Kennedy, to name a few.

With the variety of materials, styles, colors, prices, you should talk with the family funeral director in your area. They will be happy to explain everything in detail, and show you what is available in their Casket Selection Room.

The largest casket manufacturing companies in the United States, are the Batesville Casket Co. Inc.; the Aurora Casket Co. Inc., the York Group, and the Clarksburg Casket Co.

There are many other companies, too numerous to mention here. Be assured, they all do their best, to provide the best quality casket, in every price range.

Many of the employees at these casket manufacturing plants start their employment just after high school. They stay on the job, and retire after many years of dedicated service. They are true craftsmen, and take tremendous pride in their work.

If you ever have the opportunity to tour a casket manufacturing plant, especially one that specializes in wood caskets, don't pass it up. You will find it to be a very informative and rewarding experience.

Most funeral directors have a room, or rooms, with many caskets for the family to purchase, and this is referred to as the "Casket Selection Room." During the arrangement conference, we discuss the Casket Price List and the Outer Burial Container Price List.

Then the family is escorted to the Casket Selection Room, where they select the casket of their choice. The key word here, is "select." It has been the policy at our funeral home, as with many other funeral directors, to allow the family time to "select" the casket and outer burial container of their choice.

We do not sell, nor do we push or steer, families up to a more expensive casket, or outer burial container. We answer questions, and explain the differences in the various types of caskets and outer burial containers.

We don't dare take advantage of families, during these stressful times. Knowing some of these families personally, we are somewhat aware of their ability to pay for these items. Many times, we discourage families from purchasing merchandise, they might not be able to pay for, without hardship. They always thank us later.

Often we will explain the various styles, and types of caskets to the family, and then leave them alone, in the casket selection room. When they have arrived at a decision, we are called, and return to the room.

They need this time alone to discuss prices, and the various options offered to them.

Some say this is not the usual practice with funeral homes, that are owned by the Conglomerates. We have been told, by the employees of these firms, that they receive commissions on the caskets and vaults they sell, as part of their salary package.

This is illegal in many states. We recommend you be on your guard when a funeral professional uses phrases like, "you wouldn't want to bury your pet poodle in that casket", or "I think your friends would be impressed with this particular casket," or "you need to buy this casket to show the proper love and respect for your loved one."

You can bet the farm, that he or she is working on a commission, and trying to meet or exceed a quota imposed by their employer.

These people are very good at what they do, and the language might not be as blunt as we have illustrated. Just don't let someone steer you into a contract purchase, you really don't want, nor can you afford.

CEMETERIES AND MEMORIAL PARKS

THE TRADITIONAL CEMETERY:

Let's discuss the familiar traditional cemetery that we have known for many years This category would include church cemeteries, nonprofit, and municipality owned cemeteries. Also State Veterans and National cemeteries, and privately owned cemeteries.

Just think of the thousands of church affiliated cemeteries that dot the landscape,' throughout the countryside. You can find them located in small towns and large metropolitan areas.

They range in size from very small to extremely large, and generally have restrictions as to who may be buried within their boundaries. You or a member of your family, would be required to have membership in that particular church, or congregation. There are exceptions to the rule.

The members of the Cemetery Board, who oversee the operation of the cemetery, tend to be more compassionate, and understanding of the needs of others. Especially, the unfortunate individuals who have no family, or little or no funds available, to buy grave space.

The cemetery is laid off in parcels of graves, called Lots, or Plots. Each lot or plot contains a certain number of graves, or grave sites. This could be any number from one to several dozen.

Many years ago, it was quite common for families to purchase a large number of grave sites, to accommodate many members of their family. Families are smaller now. The kids grow up, get married, and move to other parts of the country to raise a family.

They put down roots in another part of the country, and raise a family. They purchase grave sites in their new community, to accommodate their family. However, their children grow up, and move away, and the cycle starts all over again, and again.

What results, is a large number of grave sites throughout our country, that will never be used. They are paid for, in most cases, but the family members, who they were purchased for, have moved, and purchased their own lots somewhere else.

I was talking to a funeral director back East, who has heard of a woman that was married, and widowed three times, over a span of many years. All three of her husbands were interred in Arlington National Cemetery, with the idea, that she would join her husband in that grave when she died.

Obviously, she couldn't be buried in all three graves, so at the time of her death she was buried beside her first husband. This presents a serious problem for these huge cemeteries like Arlington, or any cemetery for that matter. They accumulate a large number of grave sites, that probably wol1't be used. The people who intended to use them, are buried someplace else.

In most cases a monument is located on that lot, engraved with a family name. This makes the empty graves in that lot, worthless to other families.

Quite a few people feel that we are running out of available space to bury our dead. We can't speak for all sections of our country. When we discussed this concern with cemeterians, they told us that there is plenty of space available. With prudent utilization and wise planning, we will have plenty of burial space available for the future.

Many cemeteries are, and have been encouraging multi-depth interments. With the purchase of a single gravesite, several individuals can be buried on top of each other.

We understand that many of the large cemeteries in metropolitan areas like New York City, have utilized multi-depth burials for years. There are restrictions as to the size of the caskets in these situations, but that is understandable.

Some cemeteries today, are buying back grave sites within their cemetery. They buy them from families who originally bought large numbers of graves, they no longer need. It is a simple matter to move monuments, or grave markers a few feet, to free up these spaces.

The paperwork is handled by the cemetery superintendent, or one of his or her assistants. The deed to the grave is transferred to the new owner, and the money given to the original owner of the lot. Most cemeteries charge a small fee for this service.

The original owner is happy. The new owner is happy. The cemetery is happy. A win win situation, and previously useless grave sites are put in use.

When you purchase a burial site at a cemetery, or memorial park, you are not purchasing the ground. You are buying "the right of interment," in that space(s), in perpetuity.

In years past, if you wanted to sell your space(s), most cemeteries, and memorial parks would not buy them back from you. It was up to you, to advertise, and sell them yourself, or transfer ownership to someone else.

Unfortunately, most cemeteries, and memorial parks, are operating under the old policy. When they start to run out of available space within their boundaries, they will probably implement the more modern approach.

Many cemeteries, large and small, have run out of space. They are so old, in some cases, that there is no one to care for the grounds. Weeds, and bushes have overgrown everything, and some of the monuments are falling down. In some areas, clubs and organizations, are jumping into action, and cleaning up the mess. A wonderful humanitarian work in progress. These folks derive a great sense of accomplishment, and fulfillment.

Other cemeteries that are filled to capacity, following decades of burials, can't expand. When the cemetery was developed a hundred or more years ago, they had lots of space. Now, housing developments, malls, and businesses have completely surrounded the cemetery.

When they can't annex adjacent land, they simply go to the suburbs, and buy large tracts of land. They develop their newly acquired property, and hire a sales force. Hopefully, they plan for the future, and utilize every square foot possible

MEMORIAL PARKS:

Talk about "a cash cow", memorial parks, are what the doctor ordered, if you want to make money, and lot's of it.

The newer memorial parks do not have upright monuments. Most have flat markers, flush with the ground. They are, in most cases, absolutely beautiful, and meticulously maintained.

Generally, they are designed to represent a "park like" setting, that is very peaceful, and tranquil. They do just that With the exception of a few religious, military, and ecological statues, flags, and monuments, you would think you are in a beautiful park.

Located within this park, you will usually find an office, a crematory, a mortuary, and possibly a mausoleum. They sell bronze markers, outer burial containers, urns, caskets, and other sundry items. Many of these items are in the high price range.

Memorial parks are divided into areas, seplucurs, gardens, lawns, pastures, yards, tracts, and sections, to name a few, that are designated by various names.

They are named for Christian and Hebrew symbols, Veterans, Military, Flowers. Trees, Presidents, National Heros, and the list goes on.

Most have a large sales force, usually composed of retired people, housewives, teachers, etc. whom they train. They maintain a sales program, which includes mailing brochures, door-to-door canvasing, and telemarketing.

The sales force is trained to be very aggressive, not to take no for an answer. For example. Our staff hairdresser and her husband were visited by one of these salesman, on a Friday night, around 7 p.m. at their residence.

The salesman was very polite, but very insistent. At one in the morning, our hairdresser called me at home. She said "she didn't want to be rude, but this guy did not know what the word no, meant". She asked me what to do.

I told her to sign the contract, which was for two graves, two concrete liners, and a bronze companion marker, for she and her husband. She said, "we can't afford these things. He want's us to sign a contract for almost seven thousand dollars."

I repeated my recommendation, to sign the contract. Our state has a law, which allows a person to rescind, or cancel a signed contract, within three business days.

She understood immediately. She informed me later, that she and her husband signed the contract, and the persistent salesman left their house, around one thirty a.m.

Monday morning, she and her husband, marched into the sales office at the memorial park, and canceled their contract. She was very happy, but the Memorial Park people were not.

When she arrived at my office, we explained some things to her, that really opened her eyes.

1-lad she purchased two graves at one of the local cemeteries in our city. Bought two outer burial containers from a funeral home Plus purchasing a monument from a local monument dealer, she would have saved several thousand dollars.

Quite a difference. As shocking as it sounds, it is a true story.

Some memorial parks now require the family to pay all opening and closing charges, 48 hours prior to the interment. This requires a trip to the memorial park by a member of the family. Quite an inconvenience, for a grieving family, especially if the memorial park is several miles out of town.

A superintendent of a large memorial park, told us their sales figures averaged between one hundred eighty thousand dollars and two hundred and forty thousand dollars, per month. Quite a nice cash flow. It is not surprising that the national conglomerate chains, have purchased many of these memorial parks.

Oflen a family will purchase an outer burial container from a funeral home, instead of one offered for sale at the memorial park. The memorial park charges the family an "Outer Burial Container placement fee." This fee can be one hundred dollars, or more.

It is as though the family is penalized for buying the outer burial container from someone else, and not the memorial park.

True, most all traditional cemeteries charge an "outer burial container placement fee". Normally it is one hundred dollars. It is a legitimate charge, because it takes time to place the outer burial container in the grave. We feel it doesn't have to be in the form of a penalty, to the family. Just my opinion, for what it's worth.

Memorial parks excavate a large section of land, and fill them with multiple levels of concrete boxes. These boxes or liners, are then covered back up with dirt, grass is grown on top.

These particular areas are called garden crypts, lawn crypts, or just plain crypts.

The number of levels in each grave space determines the price, which can reach several thousand dollars. This is a good plan to utilize available space.

We have had many grave side services in these crypt areas. Generally, the grave side service takes place in another area, away from the actual gravesite. This is referred to as a "mock setup",

There is a reason for this arrangement, according to employees of these memorial parks. We have been told, it is to prevent those in attendance from being subjected to any unpleasant odors, that might arise from the open crypt.

Assuming there have been one or more people previously buried in the lower levels of the crypt, the odor can be overwhelming. There is very little protection from water and underground creatures in these crypts.

In all fairness, we should mention, that the same situation could occur in a traditional cemetery. Especially, if there is a body already buried in this same grave, double deep, in a liner, and not in a vault. Another good reason to purchase a vault.

Concrete liners, are constructed similar to the crypts. They are made of concrete, reinforced with steel. Unlike vaults, they are not treated with asphalt on the outside surfaces. They are designed however, with two holes in the bottom of the liner. This allows water to drain out.

Most traditional cemeteries, insist, that the first burial in a double deep grave, be in a Burial Vault. They are constructed much heavier than concrete liners. A vault will support another outer burial container, placed on top of it, very easily

We had an interment in a memorial park this morning. It was a beautiful spring day, and the surroundings were absolutely beautiful. The trees were blooming, and the grass was lush and green. We can understand why people are pleased with their choice of burial place. It is their choice, and perhaps they don't mind paying extra for the privilege.

NATIONAL AND VETERANS CEMETERIES:

Gladstone said:" Show me the manner in which a nation or community cares for it's dead, and I will measure with mathematical exactness, the tender sympathies of its people, their respect for the law of the land, and their loyalty to high ideals."

I agree with Gladstone's assessment. All in all, our citizens do care for it's dead with great respect, and dignity. The shining star, has to be our Federal Government.

Our esteemed leaders in Washington, D.C. are well-known for fouling up most everything they attempt to do. Some say they could foul up a one horse funeral. (We will discuss that at another time, and in another book.)

However, our Federal Government is without peer, when it comes to burying our Military personnel, and our Veterans.

Our National Cemeteries are absolutely beautiful, and are sacred shrines. Also, some states have a program that created cemeteries for Veterans. These are beautiful too.

These veterans Cemeteries were created, because many people realized, that millions of our Veterans could not meet the strict requirements for burial in a National Cemetery. Also, many Veterans and their families, reside in areas far away from the nearest National Cemetery. They are reluctant to bury members of their family, in a cemetery, too far away for the family to visit regularly, and pay their respects.

We have visited many National Cemeteries, including the Punch Bowl, in Hawaii; ?? Gettysburg, PA., and Arlington, VA. Extremely beautiful and impressive. Makes you proud to be an American.

Millions of people visit our National Cemeteries each year. Many people walk among these headstones that chronicle our nations history. It's the place where we honor our countries heros, and remember the many sacrifices they made to preserve our freedom Many National cemeteries have veterans representing every war our country has fought, buried within their grounds.

While visiting the Washington, D.C. area several years ago, we were given a tour through Arlington National Cemetery. It is located across the Potomac river from our nation's capital, and established over 125 years ago.

We thought Arlington was the largest national cemetery in the country. It's not, but it is certainly the most famous. There are more than two hundred thousand veterans and their dependents buried there each year.

We were awesomely impressed by the Tomb of the Unknown Soldiers. This is referred to as the Tomb Of The Unknowns. Entombed here, under a large white sarcophagus, is the Unknown Soldier from World War I. Unknown servicemen of WWII, Korean, Vietnam also are entombed there. Symbolically, a very hallowed place of remembrance, honoring those soldiers, "Known But To God."

The Tomb is guarded 24 hours a day, everyday of the year. Regardless of weather conditions, members of the U.S. Army's 3rd Infantry, "The Old Guard" are on duty as sentinels. They are stationed at Fort Myer, VA.

When on duty, the sentinel takes 21 steps before they turn and face the Tomb for 21 seconds. This corresponds to the 21 -gun salute, our country's highest military honor. The changing of the guard is a very impressive ceremony, something each American should see. It gave us "goose bumps."

We also visited the Kennedy grave sites, where our Nations 35th President, John Fitzgerald Kennedy, was buried in 1963. His brother, Seiiator Robert F. Kennedy, was buried next to his grave in 1968. Another of our Nation's Presidents, William Howard Taft, is also buried in Arlington National Cemetery.

To complete our tour, we visited the Columbarium, located in the southeast section of the Cemetery. Eventually fifty thousand niches will be provided for cremated remains.

National, and Veterans Cemeteries have a lot in common. The grave space is provided free of charge. There is no charge for opening and closing the grave. A concrete grave liner is provided, free of charge, for the eligible veteran. The headstone, or marker is also free. There is usually a chapel, where services may be held, and there is no charge for it's use. Engraving names and dates on headstones, and markers, is also free.

National cemeteries provide Honors for deceased active duty personnel, and Veterans who meet the criteria for burial in a National Cemetery. The Honors, are performed after the religious portion of the service.

Military Honors, consist of a Chaplain, (most denominations,) and a Honor Detail. The Honor Detail includes an Officer in Charge, a Non-Commissioned Officer in Charge, Body Bearers, Rifle Detail, and Bugler. These men and women undergo rigorous training and discipline Every movement is performed with precision, and their appearance is meticulous.

Full Honors are provided for active duty and retired personnel, who meet certain criteria. Their military rank must be equivalent to a Major in the Army, or higher. This rank is apparently referred to as a "Field Grade." Full Honors include all the personnel, previously mentioned, plus a Band, a Caisson, a Riderless Black Horse, and other components.

The casket is placed on a Caisson, which is followed by a riderless black horse. Empty boots are placed backwards in the stirrups on the horse.

For General Officers, and high ranking Government officials, there are cannons, which fire away with a twenty-one gun salute.

The pageantry and reverence which takes place, is spectacular, and very impressive Of course, with both types of Honors, the casket is draped with the American flag. The flag is folded perfectly, and then presented to the next of kin, when the services are concluded.

National cemeteries will allow certain dependents to be interred in the same gravesite. This can be prior to, or after the death of the eligible spouse, or parent, if certain criteria are met. There are forms that need to be completed and signed by the primary eligible. We understand that most everything is also provided free of charge for the dependent.

The dependent is usually provided a Chaplain, and body bearers, if requested by the family. Burial space can not be reserved prior to death. Only following death will the space be assigned.

The policy pertaining to who is eligible, and who is not eligible, is clearly outlined by the National Cemetery. Please contact the superintendent's office of the National Cemetery you plan to use. The folks in these offices, are very helpful. They will answer your questions, to see if you are eligible. They will also tell you if your dependent is eligible for interment.

Most National cemeteries now provide a Columbarium, for the inurnment of cremated remains. TI1ese niches are provided free of charge. An eligible spouse or dependent can have their cremains placed in the same niche, prior to, or following the death of the eligible veteran.

The eligibility requirements for the Columbarium, are more liberal, and they extend to all honorably discharged veterans, who request inurnment in the Columbarium.

Niches in the Columbarium can not be reserved prior to death. Only after death. Here again, please contact the Superintendent's office, to request information concerning the eligibility of dependents.

Veteran cemeteries operate a little different. Everything is provided free for the eligible Veteran, but not his spouse or dependent. In these cases, the cemetery makes a charge for the concrete liner.

Veterans cemeteries usually do not provide a Chaplain, or Honor Detail. It is the responsibility of the family funeral director, to secure a clergy for the family. When the cemetery is located out of town, the Chaplain could be a Clergy person or Rabbi, who lives near the Veterans Cemetery, and provides religious services at the gravesite.

Many times, there is a funeral service at the church, or funeral home, prior to the interment at the Veterans Cemetery. If time allows, the Priest or Clergy person, who officiated at the church or funeral home, will travel to the Veterans Cemetery, for the service at the grave.

For the Military Honors, we call the American Legion, VFW or AM VETS Post, located near the Veterans Cemetery to provide a Honor Detail. In some cases, the family will need to provide their own pallbearers.

We applaud the members of these Veterans organizations, for their diligence and dedication to duty. They cheerfully take time from their busy schedules, put on their uniform, and provide a service for someone they never met. In all kinds of weather they respond to their call to duty.

They provide this impressive service willingly. Being former servicemen and service- women themselves, they are proud to serve their "Fallen Comrade," and the family members.

In some parts of our country, there are no National or Veteran Cemeteries. There might be Veterans organizations in the area, but they don't always have the people or means to provide Honors for deceased veterans. Unfortunately, many of our veterans are getting too old to serve on the Honor Details. For one reason, or another, the younger veterans are not stepping in, to continue this honorable tradition. The military bases are unable to provide personnel to honor our veterans, due to budget cuts.

Consequently, our veterans, who served their country honorably, and made sacrifices to preserve our freedom, are denied the Honors due them. A shame, and a national disgrace!!!

CITY OWNED CEMETERIES: In some cities and towns, in the United States, the cemetery is owned and operated by the local city government. The people who manage the cemetery, and take care of the grounds, are employees of the city.

Unless there is a sufficient number of burials, to pay for the operating costs, some of the city tax dollars are used to help pay the bills. Usually the fees generated by charges made made by the cemetery, to open and close the graves, and the sale of burial sites, covers most expenses. Most of the employee salaries, are paid by the city, since they work in other departments, other than the cemetery. When needed, they take care of what must be done at the cemetery.

We have had burials in several of these type cemeteries, and found everything to be very nice. They are run efficiently, and provide a very necessary service for the residents of the community.

The same is true for all of the Masonic cemeteries we have been in. They are managed by the members of the local Masonic lodge, and are operated very nicely. We are lucky to have people, and organizations such as the Masons, to care enough about people, and provide a beautiful resting place for the dead. It takes a lot of time, many people, and considerable amount of money to accomplish this task.

TYPES OF CREMATION SERVICES

IMMEDIATE OR DIRECT CREMATION:

IMMEDIATE CREMATION, or as it is referred to in some parts of the country, DIRECT CREMATION, is a method of disposition of the dead, that is growing in popularity in some areas of our country. The percentage of cremations versus traditional, and other services, varies from one geographical section of the country, to the other.

For example on the west coast, around San Francisco, approximately 50% of the dead are cremated. New England about 10%, Florida 25-35%, Middle Atlantic States, 13-18%, and in the heartland approximately 3-5%. Some areas, less than 1%. These are just approximations.

There are several reasons for its growing popularity, and depending on whom you talk to, the answers vary as much as the percentages of cremation, and the costs, thereof.

In talking with other funeral directors, clergy, and reading books published by some of our highly respected authors on the subject, we have concluded a few of the many reasons why some folks favor cremation.

1: Many religious groups have eliminated their particular objections concerning cremation, and this has added to the increase of cremation.
2: Some folks feel we are running out of grave space, and cemeteries have no room for tradition burials. In most areas of our country, this is not true.
3: Cremation is less costly than traditional funeral services, and that is an important factor for many people.
4: Some people don't like the idea of being buried underground, and others' feel that mausoleums are going to fall down someday.

Some of our leading psychologists are concerned about those individuals who choose direct or immediate cremation, only because they want to get things over quickly. The people who do not have any type of service, and the people who keep their feelings welled up inside. These are people who don't share their grief with other family members and friends.

"Grief shared is grief diminished," and believe it or not, it could prevent certain psychological problems from occurring in the future. These people who want to avoid making arrangements and participating in the grief process, are in effect, denying themselves, and other family members and friends closure.

These same psychologists strongly feel this could be the possible cause of mental health problems in the future years.

When a person dies, and the family wants Immediate/Direct Cremation, the funeral director meets with the family and secures all the information needed for the Death Certificate and the obituary in the newspaper.

During the arrangement session, your funeral director will have the next of kin sign an "Authorization for Cremation" form. If there is no family member, then an attorney, or someone who has authority to do so, will sign the form. "Power of Attorney" terminates at the tune of death, and is no longer in effect.

Most all funeral directors have this form, and will complete the necessary information required on the form. It must be signed and completed prior to cremation taking place. Basically this is a hold harmless agreement The next of kin, or the individual who has the authority to do so, directs the funeral director to transport the deceased to the Crematorium.

Also, it authorizes the Crematorium to cremate the deceased. It is also designed to protect all parties involved. Once cremation takes place, there is no turning back, or changing your mind.

Your funeral director will return the cremains (ashes) to the survivor, or the person authorized to receive them, for disposition. Most families purchase an urn, suitably constructed for: interment in a cemetery; inurnment in a columbarium or niche in a mausoleum; or displaying in their home.

Of course, if the family decides to scatter the remains, the purchase of an urn is not necessary.

If it was the wish of the deceased to have his or her cremains scattered, care should be taken to avoid scattering on private property. You must contact the owner of the property, and secure written permission prior to scattering the cremains. Cemeteries and memorial parks, as a rule, prohibit the scattering of cremains on their property.

Cremains have been scattered in a variety of places. Rose gardens, back yards, race tracks, streams, rivers, bays, oceans, mountain tops, valleys, farms and ranches. Also, favorite fishing and hunting spots and golf courses. They have been scattered out of boats, cars, trucks, airplanes, and off motorcycles.

Keep in mind, when cremains are scattered, there is no grave or monument, or marker for family and friends to visit and pay their respect. It is as though all traces of the deceased have disappeared forever off the face of the planet.

Costs vary considerably throughout the country. In the sections of the country where there is a high percentage of cremations, many funeral homes, cemeteries, and memorial parks have their own crematory. They are very competitive.

Charges for direct cremation in those areas average about $ 500.00 to $ 750.00. Some sections of the country the average cost for a cremation service is between $2,000.00 and $3,500.00. Other sections fall somewhere in between.

In addition to the charges I have mentioned, there will be an additional charge for items such as certified copies of the death certificate, and if the newspaper makes a charge, the obituary.

Some folks join a Cremation Society in their city or state., They pay a fee to join, and the society takes charge of all Immediate/Direct cremation services for their members. Charges vary throughout the country, but as a rule their charges are at the low end of the spectrum.

They also will bill you for additional items, such as certified copies of the death certificate, obituaries in the newspaper, and additional mileage to travel to the place of death.

If your particular Cremation Society serves the entire state, there may be a delay of several hours, or a day, in removing the deceased from the place of death. Generally that is not a problem, if death occurs inside. This could be a problem if death occurs outdoors. It happens.

There was a sensational news story sometime back, about a crematorium located in a large cemetery, that was co-mingling bodies in their crematory. They were cremating five or six bodies at the same time, to save operating costs. This of course is illegal, and immoral.

The newspaper stated that the identification tags (toe tags) for each body were taped to the side of the cremation furnace. Several bodies were cremated at the same time, and the ashes naturally mixed together.

The ashes were then placed in containers. The identification tag, was picked randomly, and put in the container. The ashes and the identification tags did not match.

This of course is an outrageous practice. However, who's to say this doesn't occur today? We have large Cremation Societies, other similar groups, and memorial parks with crematoriums, that specialize in cremation services, at unrealistically low prices. Do they cremate several bodies at the same time to save on operating costs? We sincerely hope not.

Remember. You get what you pay for. You must be absolutely sure that your loved one, and not someone else is in that container that was returned to you. Your family funeral director takes precautions to prevent this situation from occurring.

First, most states require funeral homes to place an identification bracelet around the ankle of the deceased. Cemeteries, Memorial Parks, and societies, are not governed by the same laws as funeral homes.

Second, the deceased is cremated at the funeral director's crematory, or is taken to a crematory that the funeral director has the utmost confidence in. Usually, this crematory is owned by a funeral home in another city.

Third, a disk, is placed with the remains, and the disk if numbered and/or has the deceased name on it. Positive identification.

Each individual body is cremated, one at a time. Your family funeral director takes this responsibility that is entrusted to him or her, very seriously. If your family funeral director would suspect any hanky-panky, they would be the first to bring charges against the crematory.

Quite often some families, for one reason or another, do not call for the cremated remains of their loved one, and just leave them with the funeral director.

We have many cremains in our funeral home, which folks have left with us, some dating back more then 50 years. We of course will continue to shelter them, free of charge, until some member of the family claims them.

Many cremains are transported from the crematory to the funeral home, cemetery, or a location in another part of the state, or country, by the United States Postal Service. They are mailed "Priority Mail" and handled with utmost dignity. This is a common practice, and has been done this way for many, many years.

MEMORIAL SERVICES:

Many families are following immediate/direct cremation, with a Memorial Service. This memorial service can be held a few days following cremation, or many weeks or months later. At a time when family members are able to travel and gather together.

Some families wish to handle all the details themselves, without the assistance of their family funeral director. This is risky in some instances, but can be done, if that is what the family wants.

It will cost a little more, but, to be assured that everything will go smoothly, it is wise to have your family funeral director in charge. He has the knowledge and experience. You only have this one opportunity for this service, and you want it done right. You can't come back next week and do it over again, because everything didn't go smoothly the first time.

Memorial services are held at churches, funeral honies, cemeteries, private homes, outdoors, activity buildings, and most anywhere that would be appropriate, and dignified.

Many times a clergy/priest are present, and family members and friends discuss fond remembrances of the deceased, followed by a period of fellowship and ref~~resl~ment. These services can be private for the family and invited close friends, or open to the general public. Music is also an important part of this service. Your family funeral director should be in charge.

Other times, there are no clergy/priest, or funeral director present. Family members and close friends handle the service, with religious readings and/or fond remembrances presented. Music, food and fellowship are an important part of this service.

We have conducted very impressive memorial services outdoors, in beautiful surroundings. Wooded areas, parks with a beautiful lake, and stone outcroppings overlooking a beautiful valley.

These locations were very meaningful to the deceased, and members of the family. You feel very close to God in these spots, and when you leave the service, you feel good. You feel much better then when you arrived.

Whether you have a religious service, or not, of course is your choice. Over the years, we funeral directors have come to realize that some type of memorial service should be held.

We see a transformation that comes over family members, following a memorial service. They are deeply touched by the presence of family and friends. Some they haven't seen for years. It has a comforting effect on them. It helps to know others genuinely care.

In attendance are co-workers, members of clubs and organizations, and old school friends of their loved one. People they don't know, or ever met. 1-lowever, these people took time to be at the service, and share their memories of the deceased.

Sometimes the friends need consoling from the members of the family. Family members are touched by the feelings shared by people that knew their loved one. It is good therapy for all concerned, to share feelings, and discuss the good times. It helps diminish the grief.

Of course, you can arrange all the details of a memorial service, without the assistance of your family funeral director. And you would be saving money by doing everything yourself.

But, have you thought of every detail? Have you done this hundreds of times before? Your family funeral director has. Your family funeral director should be present. We have the knowledge and experience, and this gives you time to visit with family and friends, and relax.

You need your funeral director's help to arrange the music and flowers, parking, and seating of guests. The funeral director and staff members, will make sure that everyone signs the register/ guest book, and receives a bulletin or memorial folder. Photos' need to be displayed properly. Last minute floral arrivals, and little problems that need attention.

A guest may arrive in a wheelchair, and need assistance. Someone faints or has a medical problem. Directions to the toilets are needed. A tactful referee is needed for family members that don't get along with each other, and quietly escort unwelcome drunks outside. There are many reasons, too numerous to mention here, why you should have your family funeral director in attendance, to guide you smoothly through this type of service.

CREMATION WITH ATTENDED RITES

For those individuals who want a traditional service, and also want to be cremated, this is for you. You can have the best of both worlds.

When you have the arrangement conference with your funeral director, ask him about Cremation with Attended Rites. Fle or she will explain everything in detail to you.

The removal is made from the place of death. The signed death certificate is secured from the attending physician. The body is embalmed, (if you want viewing), dressed, cosmetics, and placed in the casket.

Here is one of the main differences from a traditional funeral service. You don't purchase a casket. You rent it. The charge made by your funeral director for the rental casket, usually covers the expenses involved with returning the casket to the casket company, and refitting it with a new interior.

A period of visitation is held, with the casket opened or closed, whatever you choose. The other family members and friends are afforded an opportunity to pay their respects, and their condolences to the immediate family.

A funeral service is then held, at the funeral home, church, or temple. The family and friends are then dismissed, and the body is removed from the rental casket, and taken to the crematorium, for cremation. The cremains (ashes) are then disposed of according to the wishes of the deceased, and/or the family.

Unless the cremains are in interred in the ground, or placed in a niche in a columbarium or mausoleum, there would be no cemetery expenses. You don't need to purchase a grave space, or pay the opening and closing fees cl1arged by the cemetery. Neither would you need to purchase an outer burial container, such as a grave liner or a vault. You would only have the charge made by the Crematory, for the cremation.

The total cost of this type of service would be more than an Immediate/Direct cremation service, but less than a traditional service with in ground burial, or entombment in a mausoleum.

We find this type of service is being held in the evening, so that those attending the services don't need to take time off of work, and quite often the clergy are more readily available, because of their busy daytime schedules.

Cremation with Attended Rites, is growing in popularity, all across the country.

COPY OF STANDARD FORM AUTHORITY TO CREMATE

Identified by _____Signature: _____
Address:_____ Date: _____
City, State: _____ Zip: _____Relationship: _____
Time of Death _____   NUMBER

AUTHORITY TO CREMATE

No cremation shall take place until a written authority signed by the
proper relative or legal representative of the deceased has been given
to the Crematory.

The undersigned hereby requests and authorizes the above mentioned Crematory. in accordance with Its. rules and regulations, to cremate the remains of _____ who died on the_____ day of _____, 20___; and certifies that he or she has the right to make such authorization; and agrees to hold the herein mentioned Crematory and the Funeral Director, herein named, harmless; and to Indemnity them, their heirs, and assigns from any liability on account of said authorization and cremation. Funeral Home nor Crematory will not be responsible for any valuables or jewelry left on deceased.

The Crematorium takes no responsibility for cremated remains for the care of which no permanent provision is made within a period of sixty (60) days, and it is part of the terms of this authorization that the crematory may dispose of such cremated remains by any means or method, as and when convenient. The undersigned and or the heirs-at-law, either Jointly or severally, shall be held liable for rental space occupied by the remains pending the time they are permanently disposed, and for interment charges, if interred.

_____   _____ (Seal)
Witness   *Signature of Relative or Legal Representative*

_____   _____
Funeral Home   *What Relation to Deceased or Authority to sign*

_____ 20_____   _____
                                          Address

AUTHORITY TO DELIVER OR FORWARD

I do hereby request and authorize that said cremated remains of the decedent above mentioned, be delivered and/or forwarded, by any convenient means of transportation to _____ Funeral Director Other; Specify and agree to hold above mentioned Crematory harmless, and to Indemnify it, its heirs, and assigns from any liability, costs, or damages arising because of such delivery to above named party.

_____ (Seal)
                                       Signed

_____ 20 _____
                                   Relationship

RECEIPT OF DELIVERY

I do hereby acknowledge receipt of said cremated remains of the decedent, above mentioned, on this the day of_____ 20_____

_____ (Seal)
                                       Signed

_____
               Checked Out By

DONATION OF THE BODY TO MEDICAL SCIENCE

I'm referring to an individual who donates his or her complete body to the State Anatomy Board, or the State Medical School systems. These institutions receive dead human bodies for medical research, and dissection by students who are studying to become doctors, and research scientists. The name of the agencies or facilities that provide this service, may vary from state to state, but the basic procedure is similar.

If this is something you are interested in, you should discuss it with your family. If it is not possible to discuss with family members for one reason or another, then you should discuss your plans with a close friend, or your attorney. Someone other than yourself, must know your wishes.

You must make arrangements with the proper state offices, while you are still living. Seldom will Medical Schools or Anatomical Boards accept a dead body without the necessary, preliminary applications, signed by the donor, and on file in their office.

Contact the appropriate office in your state, and request an application form for Donating a Dead Human Body for Anatomical Purposes. Complete the form in its entirety, sign it, make a copy for your records, and return the original to the appropriate office.

They will issue a card to carry in your purse, or wallet, and another to put with your records and personal papers. You must let someone else know what your plans are, so that when you die, they will be able to carry out your wishes.

The Anatomy Board, and/or Medical School System has contracted with one or more individuals throughout your state to make the removal of your body from the place of death. There is no charge to you or your family for this service. You must realize, that due to the size of the geographical area these individuals cover, and depending on bow busy they are, it could take many hours, upwards to a day or more, before they can respond and remove your body. They also need to secure a death certificate signed by your attending physician, or the medical examiner/coroner if the mode of your death requires their involvement. (More on Medical Examiners and Coroners in another chapter in the book.)

Your body is then transported to the appropriate facility, and embalmed. It is retained by the Medical School or Anatomy Board, for several weeks or up to several months.

When you completed and signed your original application, you will have indicated on the form, how you want the Anatomy Board, or Medical School to dispose of your ashes when they have completed their dissection and research.

The body will be cremated, and depending on what you put on the original form, the State will do one of two things. They will bury your ashes in a "Potters Field," which is land owned by the state for the burial of the dead in unmarked graves. Or some states will return the cremains (ashes) to the person indicated on your application form, for disposition according to your wishes, in your hometown.

All services provided by the Anatomical Board or Medical School System, are usually free of charge to you, or your family.

ANATOMICAL GIFTS

A wonderful gift from one person to another. When you think of the many miracles in medicine today, where hearts, livers, skin, corneas of the eyes, bone marrow, and other types of tissue are transplanted, it is very impressive. It could be the tip of the iceberg, with many wonderful miracles to come.

Many more people are needed to participate in this program of sharing parts of their body with those who desperately need these parts to survive, or improve their quality of life.

You should contact your funeral director, who will be glad to assist you in securing the necessary forms and applications for anatomical gifts. Your family physician can assist you as well. Also, many states have a Section on the drivers license, stating you are an organ donor.

When a gift of organs and tissue is made, it may delay the funeral director in transporting the body to the funeral home. However, it normally allows for the survivors to make funeral arrangements in a timely manner. If done correctly, there should be no problem in viewing the body, if that is what the family wants.

This topic should be discussed with all members of the family, and arrangements for making an anatomical gift should be made by the donor, prior to death.

Time is a factor, as the tissues deteriorate quickly after death, and any delays could result in making the gift of tissue and organs unacceptable.

Some states have teams of professionals who travel throughout the state to harvest these tissues and they need to be notified as soon as possible.

Here again, it is important to discuss this with your family physician, and funeral director. You don't want any delays, or foul-ups when death occurs. It is very important to have all the necessary paperwork completed, and on file.

If death occurs in a hospital, it is no problem to leave the body there, in anticipation of the arrival of the professional team, to harvest the tissue and organs.

However, should death occur at a nursing center, or at the residence, your family funeral director will need to transport the deceased to the hospital, or the funeral home. The professional team will then perform their duties at the hospital or funeral home.

It is common for these professionals to arrive during the wee hours of the morning. They are busy people, and cover a large geographical area.

We have been told they make no charge for this service. This of course, could be different in your part of the country.

CERTIFIED COPIES OF THE DEATH CERTIFICATE

The funeral director completes most of the information on the death certificate, and then signs it. In the Vital Statistics section of this book, we have illustrated the information requested by the funeral director. All the information must be typed correctly and neatly.

The attending Physician, Medical Examiner, or Coroner, will fill in the cause of death, provide other information, and then sign the certificate. The funeral director will then mail or take the certificate to the Health Department.

When fully completed, and signed, it is a legal, and public document, This is the one and only, original death certificate for that particular person. The same is true for a birth or marriage certificate. The certificate is then filed with the State Department of Health.

We have many people ask us for an original death certificate. This of course is not possible, and not exactly what they need, What they need, is a certified copy of the certificate.

Since the death certificate is a public record, anyone, with a legitimate reason, can request a copy. Generally, it is the funeral director, or a member of the family who secures them.

An application form must be filled out, and accompanied with a check, made payable to the Health Department, Vital Records, or Vital Statistics Section. States have different names for the agency that handles certificates.

All states, and the District of Columbia, make a charge for each certificate issued. This charge varies greatly, from state to state. Some charge $15.00; up to $20.00 per copy. Others charge more for the first copy, and less for the additional copies, ordered at the same time. For instance, if you are ordering six copies, the first copy might be $11.00, and copies two through six, will be $2.00 each, making a grand total of $21.00.

It gets confusing, but your family funeral director knows what the charges are, and will be happy to order any number of copies for you. The same is true for Birth, Marriage, and Divorce records.

Most funeral homes will not make an additional charge, to order the copies. If you order ten copies, and the charge made by the Health Department is $50.00, that is all you will pay. We quite often order certified copies for families, whose loved one died in another state, or died many years ago.

It takes some of these states, several weeks to mail us the requested copies. This is particularly frustrating to people who suddenly find they need one or two copies, and they need them yesterday.

Most State Health Departments are located in the Capital city of that state. We contact a courier service, or a funeral home in that city, and they secure the copies for us, in a few days. They do make a charge for this service, maybe $10.00, and the cost of the certificates.

Many states started collecting Vital Records, many years ago. I believe, Massachusetts has records, back to the late 1600's, and Boston city records start in 1649. Also, after a death certificate has aged 20 or more years, they are transferred to another state department, e.g., The State Archives. You might have to pay more for copies of these older certificates, and wait a little longer to get them.

We will list some of the reasons, for which you will need a certified copy of a death certificate. As previously stated in the Vital Statistic section of this book, those agencies requesting a copy are assuming all information contained therein, is accurate. If not, you might have difficulty in receiving benefits from Insurance, and other agencies. With the assistance of your funeral director, corrections can be made, but this is not an easy process. You might need copies for: Insurance policies

Real Estate Deeds
Stocks and Bonds
Savings, Checking accounts, and Certificates of Deposit
Banks and other Financial institutions
Mortgage loans that will be paid off by credit life insurance
Credit Cards with credit life insurance
Veterans Administration (One or more copies provided free of charge)
Loans for Vehicles, Appliances, Furniture, etc. with credit life insurance
Trust Agreements
Conservatorship, and Guardianship
Retirement plans, and Annuities (might need more than one copy)
Personal Notes
Some Orphans Courts, and Register of Wills
Genealogy

This is a partial list to give you an idea of how vital these certificates are, especially in settling some deceased persons estates. We recommend you refer to the Vital Statistics section of this book, and itemize your particular needs. Write them down, and as the years pass, make corrections and additions. You will make probating your estate much easier for your heirs.

Many airlines will offer compassionate fares, for family members traveling to a relatives funeral service. They might need a copy of the death certificate, which your funeral director can provide for you. It does not have to be a certified copy.

PALLBEARERS

A pallbearer is an individual who helps carry or transport a casket or container, containing human remains. In some parts of the country, they are referred to, as bearers, or casket bearers.

This is a time-honored tradition, and to be asked by the family to serve as a pallbearer, is a distinct privilege. Bearers may be male or female, family members, friends, lodge members, business associates, fellow employees, or anyone the family wishes.

Military organizations, police departments, and fire companies, often have personnel trained to provide this service, on a regular basis. They do a great job, and are quite impressive.

The day we toured Arlington National Cemetery, we had the honor to witness a U. S. Marine Corps Honor Detail during a grave side service. Over the years, I have personally witnessed thousands of pallbearers remove a casket from the hearse. The loving, caring manner employed by the Marines, that day, brought tears to my eyes.

All six of these tall, strong, impeccably dressed Marines, slowly approached the rear of the open hearse. Just as two marines reached into the hearse to remove the casket, the other four, slowly bent forward. They extended their arms forward, with hands cupped up, as if to say, "don't worry comrade, you will be safe in our hands."

This scene portrayed the many times in combat, the men and women of our armed forces, while in harms way, reached to help a fallen, or wounded comrade. The symbolism portrayed by the Marines that day, was very touching.

Many police and firemen, carry the casket, by placing it high up on their shoulders. This is a very old tradition, and is not easy to perform. They deserve a lot of credit, for this impressive procedure.

If you are going to serve as a pallbearer, and have not done so previously, don't worry, it's not that difficult. Generally, you will be required to wear a suit and tie.

It is important you arrive at the site of the funeral, 30 to 45 minutes prior to service time. Most pallbearers drive their own cars, and can take the members of their respective family with them. Some bearers will ride to the cemetery with other bearers. The pallbearers' car(s), will usually be put in a special place, if there is a procession to a cemetery. This will be in front of the hearse, and behind the car that will transport the clergyperson, or lead the procession.

The funeral director will show you where you will sit, in the funeral home, with the other bearers, After the funeral is over, you might be asked to help carry flowers to the flower van. The bearers, will then carry the casket, place it carefully in the hearse, and go to their cars.

When the procession arrives at the final destination, the bearers will report to the rear of the hearse. The casket is carried to the gravesite, and placed carefully on a lowering device. The bearers, then join their family, or perhaps form a semicircle near the casket.

When the service is at a church, the bearers may carry the casket into the church, or the funeral director, and staff, may have taken care of this earlier. The funeral director, or an assistant, will escort the bearers in a group, to the pew or pews, they will occupy.

When the service is concluded, the Clergy will exit first, followed by the bearers, who will wait at the outside door for the casket. The funeral director, and a staff member, will bring the casket to the bearers, and they will carry it to the hearse. The bearers then go to their cars, and the procession will travel to the gravesite.

There are exceptions to these procedures, too numerous to mention. One that comes to mind, is a Mass at a catholic church. Other religious denomination has slight variations to the procedure. The funeral director will explain everything in detail.

If the Mass is scheduled for 10:00 a.m. at the church, you might be asked by the funeral director, to report to the funeral home, as early as 8:00 a.m. This depends on how long it takes to drive to the church. The bearers carry the casket from the funeral home, and place it carefully in the hearse. The funeral procession travels to the church, and the bearers follow the procedure for a church funeral, as described previously. When the Mass is over, the procession proceeds to the gravesite for burial. When services are held at church, often the bearers are called upon to serve both at the funeral home and the church.

There are many exceptions to the procedures we have listed, and customs vary greatly from state to state. We have listed a few of the basic procedures for you.

If you are ever asked to serve as a pallbearer, and you are able to, don't hesitate to do it. It is an honor to serve in this capacity, and it will be greatly appreciated by the family. The funeral director will guide you through it.

As a rule, Honorary Pallbearers don't actually carry the casket. Theirs is a position of honor, and they serve in a capacity of an honor guard, or honor detail. Some Honorary bearers may have physical problems, which will allow them to be present at the service, but will not allow them to lift or carry much weight. They usually line up, in formation, or ranks, and the active bearers carry the casket between them, as they leave the church, and as they approach the grave.

CONGLOMERATES AND INDEPENDENT FUNERAL HOMES

There has been a significant increase in recent years in the growth of several large corporations, which have purchased hundreds of independent funeral homes, cemeteries, crematories, casket manufacturers, chemical companies, pre-funded funeral plans, monument companies, florists, and companies that manufacture supplies and merchandise used by funeral homes. This large interstate, and in some cases international, corporation is referred to as a CONGLOMERATE.

What is the purpose of this huge corporation? The pooling of funeral home personnel, motor equipment, the purchasing of caskets, vaults, and other merchandise used by funeral homes, in large volume, and at a lower cost. Do they pass these savings onto the consumer? Some people say no.

There are several of these huge groups out there, competing with each other in the acquisition of independently owned funeral homes, and cemeteries, etc. So many in fact that at the National Funeral Directors Association annual conventions, you can't help but notice all the booths in the Exhibition Hall rented by these huge corporations. They are there to meet the thousands of funeral directors attending the convention, and to talk to them about buying their funeral homes, cemeteries, and crematories.

Also, there are several booths rented by large companies that will assist you in selling your funeral home to these conglomerates. For a fee, these folks will appraise your funeral home and business, and assist you in securing the best possible price if you sell to the conglomerate. Certainly is a big change in our funeral service industry, and unfortunately, a sign of the times.

There is no doubt in my mind, that our grandparents and parents, who founded our independent businesses, would roll over in their graves, if they knew what was happening now.

I'm not telling you that this is all bad. However, there is much to be said about the independent, family owned funeral home, that we have all been accustomed to. The folks you have grown up with, those who have been an integral part of your community, and have guided you through some of the worst times of your life. You know who I mean. The man or woman who you entrusted your deceased loved one to, and who did their very best to provide the finest service available Your independent family funeral director.

In large metropolitan areas, some of these corporations own most of the funeral homes, within a short distance of each other. This is referred to as "clustering" I heard a story about a gentleman who made an appointment with a funeral home to discuss pre-need arrangements. The funeral director he met with, was very polite, and explained everything in detail. He did however, give the impression, here it is, take it or leave it. The gentleman thought it might be wise to consult another funeral home in the same area.

This gentleman, as the story goes, went home, and made an appointment for the next morning at another funeral home, in the same area of the city. When he arrived at this funeral home the next morning, much to his surprise, sitting behind the desk, was the same funeral director he bad visited the previous day.

The funeral director explained that he and other employees were shuttled from one firm to another. He received a copy of this firm's price list, and it was identical to the price list he received the previous day.

The gentleman made inquires, and located an independently owned funeral home. He made an appointment to meet the next morning.

He was pleasantly surprised to find that all his questions could be answered on the spot. The funeral director explained, that since he was a staff member of the funeral home, and acting on behalf of the owner, he could accommodate the gentlemen in ways that the conglomerate firms could not. Also, since his price list showed that his prices were much lower, he could provide some services at a lower price, or make no charge for some services, or merchandise, if it would help the family. He further explained, that be and his boss made the decisions, and did not have to abide by rules, prices and other regulations, dictated by a corporation whose headquarters were located in a far distant state.

It has also been brought to our attention, that these conglomerates fire employees that have many years of service, apparently to make room for younger recent licensed morticians. These young folks, who have little or no experience, are paid much less than those licensed people they replace. I would think most families would rather be serviced by an independent funeral borne, who have trained, and retained their staff members over a period of years. People who know how to handle difficult situations, because they have experienced them many times before. Of course, this is just my opinion, and I'm sure a representative of a conglomerate could give you many reasons why you should call his firm.

Our firm is independently owned Since we don't own several branch locations, or own a cemetery, or a crematory, I don't think the conglomerates will be interested in buying our firm.

We are called frequently by funeral directors in other states, to help them with a person who has died in our area. The first question they ask, is "are you an independent funeral home?" They know, that since we are independently owned, they will be treated fairly. The way they want to be treated.

We do the same thing, when we need the services of a funeral home in another state. The firms that are owned by these large corporations know who their counterparts are in other states. They have a list of their sister firms, and that is who they call. It's important to the families we serve, that we get the best service 'for them, at the best price.

Quite a few independently owned firms, are advertising in our national directories, and other publications and newspapers, that they are independently, or family owned. Not many people are aware of the changes in the funeral service industry. You of course, have purchased our book, and we have made you aware of your options. You can now make your decision, based on the information provided to you. An educated consumer is a smart consumer.

Many years ago, George Washington was doing some surveying for the Continental Congress. Upon completion, he submitted his bill to Congress, in the amount of $200.00. This was a lot of money in the 1700's, and Congress was not happy with his bill.

They wrote to Mr. Washington, and asked him to itemize his statement of charges. The father of our country itemized his bill, and sent it back to the Congress. It read as follows: "$5.00 for wooden stakes, $195.00 for knowing where to put the wooden stakes. Total $200.00."

Knowledge and experience, is what you should expect from your family funeral director. You are paying him/her, to know what to do in your particular situation.

Here again, I stress the importance of pre-planning. Call the funeral homes in your area and ask them questions. Ask for their price list. Ask them to explain their different types of services. Of course there are times when the funeral director might be busy with another family. If that is the case, leave your name and number, and ask them to call you later, or ask when you can call him/her later. There is no obligation, so don't hesitate to leave your name and number.

if they blow you off, hesitate to answer your questions, or refuse to mail you a copy of their price list, you might want to put them at the bottom of your list.

On the other hand, if they do call you back, if they seem genuinely interested in addressing your concerns, and mail you a copy of their price list, you might want to put them at the top of your list.

I should explain that some funeral homes hesitate to mail their price list to you. The Federal Trade Commission rules do give the funeral homes the option, when it comes to mailing the price list. These firms will ask you to come to their office, and they will be happy to give you a copy of their price list. By doing this, they are complying with the FTC Rule.

Many funeral homes are reluctant to mail their price list, because the caller might be requesting the price list for another funeral home in the area. This is a common practice in all areas of our country.

Our policy is to mail our price list to anyone who has taken the trouble to call, and ask for it. If it falls into the hands of our many competitors, so be it. I'm sure this has happened many times. We feel that our prices are fair, and we are not afraid for our competition to know what we charge. The important thing is our service, which has been the key to our success over the past decades. This is true with most independently owned funeral homes, and is the main reason families trust them, and have the confidence to call them time after time.

VETERANS BENEFITS

On a separate page in this book, we have listed the dates of the Wars the United States has been involved in, starting with World War I.

Each war has a beginning date, and an ending date, with the exception of the Gulf War. Congress will determine the date when this war will end.

One of the reasons for these dates, is to determine if a veteran is eligible for certain benefits. We have been told by the Veterans Service officer in our area, that the veteran only has to serve one day in a particular war, to meet this part of the eligibility requirements.

The most important requirement, is the veteran must have received a discharge, other than dishonorable. What do they mean by that?

We all know what a dishonorable discharge is. If the veteran has received this type of release from the military, he or she will not receive any benefits in the future.

There are several types of discharges from military service. The most desirable would be an honorable discharge. You also have medical, and mental discharges, and convenience of the (branch of service is used here), e.g., Army or Navy, etc., discharge.

If a veteran has received one of these types of discharges, we have been told that he or she could be eligible for certain benefits.

We won't get into all the ramifications of medical, mental, or convenience discharges. We recommend you contact your local Veterans Service officer for help in these matters.

What we are interested in, are the types of benefits a deceased veteran could receive, if all criteria have been met for eligibility.

There was a day and time, when all eligible veterans would receive $300.00 as a plot allowance, and $150.00 as a death benefit. This totaled $450.00. Thanks to our distinguished member of congress, this is no longer true.

To be eligible for the $450.00, it would be necessary for the veteran to die in a Veterans Administration Medical Center (VAMC); or another facility where the Veterans Administration has placed the veteran. If the VAMC is full, or the veteran's medical condition would require long term care, they are placed in a nursing facility, under the auspices and direction of the V.A. Veterans are also eligible, if they die while traveling to the VAMC for authorized treatment.

Also, if the veteran was receiving a monthly benefit check from the Veterans Administration (VA), they could be eligible for the $450.00 The monthly benefit might be as little as $6.00, for the veteran to meet the eligibility requirements.

When a veteran dies in a VAMC, the VA will pay for additional services. If the funeral bill is paid in full, the family will receive the check, if not the funeral home will receive the check. It takes three or four months for the check to be issued from the Veterans Administration. Because of the length of time it takes for the check to be issued, most funeral homes will require the family to pay the bill in full. The check in most cases will be issued to the family.

Your family funeral director will mail a copy of the itemized funeral bill to the Veterans Administration, in an effort to secure any monetary benefits for the family. A certified copy of the death certificate will be mailed with the bill, along with copy of the Discharge Papers, and/or a copy of a government form referred to as a DD2 14.

When the death has occurred in a VAMC, or VA approved nursing home facility, the VA will pay for the removal charge from the place of death to the funeral home, including any reasonable mileage charges. The charge for the use of the hearse to the cemetery or mausoleum will be also be paid, and any reasonable mileage charge. All these reasonable transportation charges could be paid, and the $450.00.

Veterans who are receiving a disability check each month, could be eligible for the $450.00. Veterans who do not receive a disability check each month, will not receive the $450.00 For the veteran to be eligible for any additional payments for removal, mileage, or hearse charges, they must die in a VAMC, or a VA designated nursing type facility.

ALL veterans, whether they receive any monetary benefits, or not, are eligible for an American Flag, and a grave marker provided free of charge. They are also eligible for burial in a Veterans cemetery, and some National cemeteries.

Gets confusing doesn't it? Well there is another matter to be considered. If the veteran is buried in a National or Veterans cemetery, they will not receive the $450.00. This is only fair, since the veteran is given a free grave space, a free concrete grave liner, and there is no charge for the opening or closing of the grave. If these items were paid by the family, they could total up to $1700.00 or more.

In summary, most veterans are not receiving a monthly disability check, and they will not receive any money from the VA. These veterans could be eligible for burial in a National or Veterans cemetery, and will receive a free grave marker, and American flag.

Vets receiving a monthly disability check will receive the $450.00, if they are not buried in a National or Veterans cemetery. They will receive a free grave marker, and American flag.

Veterans who die in a VAMC, or VA designated nursing facility will receive removal, mileage, and hearse charges. If they are not buried in a National or Veterans cemetery, they will receive $450.00. They will also receive a free grave marker, and American flag.

Many funeral directors will have you sign the various veterans forms. They will then type in the information needed, with information gathered from the Discharge Paper. Another important government form is the DD214, which contains a lot of information needed for the Veterans Forms.

Most government forms have a form designation number, listed on the bottom left corner of the form. Keep all Discharge Papers, and other important government forms, such as the DD214, in a safe place. Let your family members, know where they are.

The most commonly used forms for receiving benefits from the VA, will be provided by your family funeral director. Feel free to sign these forms, so the funeral director can mail them to the Veterans Service officer. If the funeral director will not help you with these forms, contact your local American Legion Post, or similar Veterans' organization for assistance.

One form will give the Veterans Service officer, a limited power of attorney, pertaining to veterans' affairs. Another, will be the application for benefits, if the veteran is eligible.

There is an application form for the American flag, and a form for the free grave marker. It takes a good deal of time to execute these forms, and most funeral directors will complete them for the family, as part of his basic service.

VETERANS BENEFITS

TO RECEIVE MEDICAL CARE AND CERTAIN BENEFITS FROM THE VETERANS ADMINISTRATION, WARTIME SERVICE IS REQUIRED.

WAR PERIODS RECOGNIZED BY THE VETERANS ADMINISTRATION:

Mexican Border Period---May 9, 1916 through April 5, 1917, for veteran who served in Mexico, on its borders or in adjacent waters.

World War 1--April 6, 1917, through Nov. 11, 1918; for veterans who served in Russia, April 6, 1917 through April 1, 1920; extended through July 1, 1921, for Veterans who had one day of service between April 6, 1917, and Nov. 11, 1918.

World War II--Dec. 7, 1941, through December 31, 1946.

Korean (War) Conflict--June 27, 1950, through Jan. 31, 1955.

Vietnam Era--Aug. 5, 1964, through May 7, 1975.

Persian Gulf War--Aug. 2, 1990, through a date to be set by law or Presidential Proclamation.

(*Courtesy of the Veterans Administration*)

The veteran must have received a discharge other than dishonorable.

Those Veterans who receive a monthly check from the Veterans Administration, due to a service connected disability, are eligible for additional benefits. The benefit depends on the type and severity of the disability.

Also, the Veteran could be eligible for burial in some National or Veterans Cemeteries, if space is available.

The Veteran is also eligible to receive a free grave marker, and American flag.

It is important to check with your local Veterans Service Officer, to discuss your individual situation. You might be eligible for benefits, which you are not aware of.

SOCIAL SECURITY BENEFITS

Quite often during the arrangement conference, we reluctantly have to tell the family that their loved one is not eligible to receive any money from the Veterans Administration. A look of disbelief is on their face, and they are obviously quite disappointed.

The same is true, when we tell some families, that no money will be forthcoming from the Social Security Administration, in the form of a one time, lump sum payment. The famous $255.00 lump sum death benefit.

As a rule of thumb, to be eligible, the deceased must have paid into Social Security, for a certain number of quarters during their lifetime. They must have a surviving spouse, in most cases, living under the same roof. Or they must have minor children up to 18 years of age, or older if attending an approved institution of higher learning.

The Social Security Administration, has a billion rules to govern them. Social Security manuals of survivor benefits, are extremely large, and very difficult to understand. The best advice we can give families, is to tell them to visit their local Social Security office, a week or so after the funeral.

You might call the office, and try to make an appointment Otherwise, visit the office, take a number, and expect to be there a long time. Be sure to take as many papers and documents as you can find, to help your cause. They will have most everything they need on their computers.

Your family funeral director will complete a special form that is mailed to the local Social Security office. This form will notify Social Security, that your loved one has died. It will enable them to start their procedures, to determine if you are eligible for the lump sum death benefit. It will also put a stop to the monthly Social Security check your loved one received on the first of each month.

Most of these checks are deposited directly into the individuals bank account. If a check is inadvertently deposited directly into the bank account, after death, don't touch it, and don't spend it. You might be required to return this money to the Social Security Administration. The same would be true if you received the check in the mail after death. You might be required to return the check.

As confusing as this is, generally you will find the Social Security representative very knowledgeable, and most helpful. They will correct your problems, and explain in detail, all of your questions.

Your monthly annuity, if you are receiving one, might be increased by transferring money from your deceased spouse's annuity account to your monthly check. Good Luck!

QUICK LIST OF MONEY SAVING TIPS

When ordering flowers for funerals, buy a table arrangement, vase, or garden dish from the florist. They last longer, and the family members are more apt to take it home with them.

If you are making a choice between a basket and a paper Mache container, get the paper Mache. A $100.00 paper Mache container, will have more flowers in it, than a $100.00 basket arrangement. You are paying more for the container when you get a basket.

Drive your own cars in the funeral, to avoid paying for a limousine. After the services at the grave, you will have your own transportation, and be able to go wherever you want.

If you really don't want visitation the night before the funeral, request visitation one hour prior to the funeral service. You are already paying for the use of the facility for the day of the funeral, and there should be no additional charge for this period of visitation. The same is recommended is you are having a church service. You will save the charge made for the use of the funeral home facility, the night prior to the funeral.

Use the deceased's own clothing, instead of purchasing new apparel. If the man never wore a suit, or tie, use an open collar, and sports jacket. If the lady always wore a pants suit, or sweater, that will be just fine. Pajamas and robe are very nice for women.

When ordering certified copies of the death certificates, it's a good idea to get at least two more copies than what you think you will need. It will save you a lot of frustration, months, or years, after the funeral.

Many older folks, escape the winter weather, by living in a community down south. If a loved one dies in this retirement area, and you plan to have a service and burial in your hometown, it is advisable to call your hometown funeral home. He can handle everything for you, and avoid duplication of costs. Don't let anyone talk you into a visitation in the retirement area, unless you think it will be a practical thing to do.

If a family member dies, when they are traveling out of town, always call your hometown funeral home. It will save you lots of money.

Be wary of a funeral director who tends to suggest that you buy a more expensive casket, or more expensive vault, unless there is a definite need for the same.

As we have suggested many times in this book, please take time to make pre-arrangements for yourself, and other family members. You will be in a much better frame of mind to make practical decisions.

Pay for the prearrangements, in full, if you can, and the cost will be locked-in at today price. When death occurs years in the future, and services cost more, your arrangements will already be paid in full.

When ordering a spray of flowers for on the casket, (Casket Spray), try the seasonal colors, e.g., Fall, Spring & Summer These colors are lovely for anytime of the year. Roses are very beautiful, but can be expensive. The Fall colors will be the rich deep rusts, oranges, reds, and yellows. The Spring and Summer colors will be the bright pastels. Red and white carnations, with Baby's Breath is a lovely arrangement, and usually is very reasonable in price.

Paid obituaries in Metropolitan newspapers can be very expensive. Have your funeral director condense the information as much as possible. Most of these papers charge by the line, and it doesn't take too many words and names to get the cost over $160.00 to $200.00.

Ask your family funeral director to take a lot of the flowers from the funeral home, to nursing homes, after the funeral services are over. The flowers will not last long at the cemetery, and this will bring a little sunshine into the lives of the nursing home residents. Most funeral homes will provide this service for no extra charge.

If you plan to pay the entire funeral bill in full by the day of the funeral, or shortly tl1ereafter, ask the funeral director what the discount would be for early payment. Some funeral homes require payment in full by the day of the funeral. If that is the case, they most likely do not offer a discount.

If you are appointed Power of Attorney for someone, that authority terminates at the death of the individual. In most cases, you will not be allowed to write checks, and pay for the funeral costs, until you or someone else is appointed Executor, or Personal Representative by the courts. If death is eminent, some recommend you meet with the funeral director, and prepay the funeral bill in full, prior to the individuals death.

Keep in mind when you are purchasing a casket for a loved one, you should not let your emotions cloud your better judgment. Naturally, everyone would like to get the very best, but when it comes time to pay for these items, you might find it difficult to do.

Speaking for myself, and many of the independent funeral home owners, I know, we tactfully try to discourage families from overspending. This avoids embarrassing situations after the funeral, when it is time to pay the funeral bill. Many families thank us, for helping them avoid this pitfall. You will find that most funeral homes provide the best quality available, in each price range.

Everyone's situation is a little different. If you have any peculiar problems, or you have a question you would like to ask, please write to me. Our address is located on the Quick Order Forms in the back of this book. I will do my best to respond quickly. If I don't know the answer to your particular question, I will try to find the answer for you. Of course, there is no charge for this service. Write to me, and let us know if the information in this book has been of help to you.

Printed in the United States
by Baker & Taylor Publisher Services